Pelican Books

The Peasants of North Vietnam

Gérard Chaliand, who is a French citizen, is a history
teacher and specialist in underdeveloped countries. He
was born in Brussels in 1934, and studied at the National
School of Oriental Languages in Paris. Formerly editor
and assistant manager of the Algerian weekly *Révolution
Africaine* (1963), Gérard Chaliand is the author of
L'Algérie est-elle socialiste? (1964) and *Lutte armée
en Afrique* (1967; *Armed Struggle in Africa*, 1969).
In October–November 1967 he made a study of
several villages in North Vietnam, and on his
return published a report in the *Monde
Diplomatique*. Between the years 1952–62 and
1966–9 he travelled extensively in Africa, Latin America,
the Middle East and South-east Asia.

Gérard Chaliand

The Peasants of
North Vietnam

With a preface by Philippe Devillers
Translated by Peter Wiles

 Penguin Books

Penguin Books Ltd, Harmondsworth, Middlesex, England
Penguin Books Inc., 7110 Ambassador Road, Baltimore, Maryland 21207, U.S.A.
Penguin Books Australia Ltd, Ringwood, Victoria, Australia

Les Paysans du nord-vietnam et la guerre first published by F. Maspero 1968
This translation first published in Pelican Books 1969
Reprinted 1970
Copyright © Librairie François Maspero, 1968
Translation copyright © Penguin Books Ltd, 1969

Made and printed in Great Britain by
Hazell Watson & Viney Ltd., Aylesbury, Bucks
Set in Monotype Plantin

Contents

Preface

by Philippe Devillers

What can explain the extraordinary resilience with which Vietnam is countering the pressure of the American war machine? How has this nation of thirty-two million men, women and children, poor and more or less unindustrialized, managed to survive the torrent of fire and steel to which it has been subjected for nearly eight years by the most formidable military apparatus the world has ever known? This is the question which Gérard Chaliand set out to answer during a visit to Vietnam in the autumn of 1967 – a visit largely devoted to a study of the rural communities.

The material which he brought back, and which he has deliberately chosen to publish with a bare minimum of editing, throws a remarkably revealing light on the Vietnamese people's capacity for resistance. It shows how the individual on the spot is standing up to the war – what he thinks about it, what impact it has had on him, and what keeps him going. His material and cultural background is described too.

To my mind, the most significant point to emerge from this set of documents is the remarkable 'deep-rootedness' of the men and women of the Vietnamese countryside and the manner in which the American aggression can be seen to relate to them in time and space. That aggression takes on its full historical dimension in these interviews – a dimension which it will probably retain, whatever else may happen. In the two-thousand-year-old struggle of the Vietnamese people, it stands in line with the great Chinese, Mongol and French invasions, all of which were smashed in the end, though sometimes at a terrible price. Whoever the invader may have been at a particular time, it has been one long, continuous fight for national independence and freedom from oppression. Today, great heroes of the past who won victories over mighty foes – Le Loi and Nguyen Trai, for example – are called to mind, not only to inspire confidence and determination, but to fill everyone with the resolve to match the achievements of earlier times. To remain free, to survive as a free people, to defend the nation's ancient and modern heritage: these are the basic objectives. How puny, in comparison, seem the ideological pretexts with which the Anglo-Saxons seek to slander the victims of their expansionism.

Two of the comments reported by Gérard Chaliand are very significant in this respect. One peasant says: 'The Americans are grabbing Vietnam's resources in the South and destroying everything we have built in the North. They're doing it because they want to be masters of the world. They must be driven out at all costs.' And another, a Catholic living in the district of Phat Diem: 'The Americans are cruel, very cruel. They are out to conquer our country so that they can rule it in their own way. Already they are in the South, and beyond any doubt they mean to invade us from the skies. Sooner or later they will be beaten, though.' Has anyone ever conveyed the essence of a major conflict in so few and such simple words?

Another equally fundamental point emerges from these pages. The Pentagon wrongly imagined that escalation would bring chaos to North Vietnam; instead, exposure to the furnace has considerably strengthened the nation's institutions. The 'patriotic war' has completed the task of uniting the population in a common effort. It has finally bridged the gap between the generations, between the social classes, between the main ethnic group and the minorities, between the Party organizations and the workers, whatever their background, their religious faith or their political loyalties. Events have brought the Vietnamese people to a new level of consciousness in which nationalism, democracy and socialism merge and interact to an even greater degree than before.

In North Vietnam, government and Party have succeeded –

more quickly, more sincerely and more effectively, it would seem, than in any other socialist country – in identifying Marxism with the national heritage. The political successes which they have reaped since they placed national independence in the forefront of their aims are ample testimony to the truth of this statement. A nation is the product of a long process of material, intellectual and spiritual accumulation. It is the end-product of numberless individual and collective contributions, of a sustained experience of human beings and environment, of techniques painstakingly evolved and discerningly applied. In short, it is the holder of a legacy which each new generation must hand on to the next, after imprinting it with their own labours. This is especially true of a rural community, where man is living at once in conflict and in harmony with nature.

Why throw away the advantages of this legacy merely to satisfy the rules of a narrow, inflexible dogmatism ? By restoring the concept of 'the people, makers of history' to its original place of prominence, socialism is able to take over all that is worth preserving in the country's heritage, and to ensure the continuity of the popular and national effort.

Readiness to inherit and reinvigorate the existing collective institutions of the nation – in particular, the rural communities – has made it possible for socialism to turn the country into a genuine 'confederation of villages', which even the most modern methods of warfare have been powerless to dismember. To the astonishment of those who did not know Vietnam, these thousands of living cells – enjoying a broad measure of autonomy and drawing their essential nourishment from the land and water – have held firm in spite of the terrorism to which they have been subjected from the air. Far from disintegrating, they have derived a new vitality from the change in the patterns of production and from the increasing democratization. One can only hope that this new vitality will survive the war and any future return to bureaucratic Communism. Certainly it has led to victory in the battle of production, but for which all the rest might have been in vain.

Peasant communities versus modern warfare . . . Gérard Chaliand prompts us to reflections on this theme which extend far beyond the framework of the conflict which inspired his visit and, in turn, this book.

PHILIPPE DEVILLERS

9 July, 1968

for Juliette

Author's Preface

This book is the outcome of a five-week tour of inquiry among the villages of three provinces in the Red River delta (formerly known as the Tonkin delta), carried out during October and November|1967. The area is the most densely populated region of the Democratic Republic of Vietnam, containing 75 per cent of the national population.

Preceded by a sketch-history outlining the basic social facts about Vietnam past and present, this sociological and economic survey may be regarded as a documentary dealing with the Vietnamese people at the time of the escalation of the Vietnam War – though in fact it has a wider scope, giving the inside story of the D R V from colonial times to the present, as experienced by the Vietnamese peasants and by the political and administrative cadres working in contact with the grass roots.

Escalation has not brought about the collapse of the Democratic Republic of Vietnam, even though the United States has – on her own admission – dropped nearly seven hundred thousand tons of high explosives since 1965. How has a small agricultural land, with nothing in its favour save determination and ingenuity, managed to stand up to the nation which leads the world in technological achievement?

The answers to this question can be arrived at only through a first-hand knowledge of the facts about the Vietnamese countryside. There are historical reasons, stemming from the inherited patterns of Vietnamese rural society, and political reasons, stemming from those later patterns which the regime has deliberately fostered. The survival of North Vietnam has been made possible by massive decentralization, a wholesale movement away from the towns and cities; the process has been facilitated by the communal traditions of village life and carried out with a remarkable degree of technical efficiency. Escalation, an attempt to weaken the South by battering the North, has clearly failed in its purpose; otherwise the offensive which began early in February 1968 could never have been launched.

The Red River delta is the key, life-supporting region of North Vietnam; that is why it was chosen as the setting for the present survey. So long as the economic life of the villages in the delta is not basically disrupted, North Vietnam's survival is assured – and in this respect escalation has failed completely. The provinces in which my inquiries were carried out are: Hung Yen, a region enjoying average economic success; Thai Binh, an area with a much higher yield; and Ha Tay, an in-between zone, geographically on a level with the highlands (the economy of Ha Tay is not purely agricultural; local handi-crafts are an important factor). A few pages are devoted to the province of Nin Binh, at the extreme southern end of the delta; but in this case I can only record what I heard as I was passing through.

I should like to express my admiration for the energy and imaginativeness of the Vietnamese people, and for their excep-tional capacity for hard work and thorough organization. For me, these qualities were perfectly summed up in a slogan I saw displayed in one of the villages: 'Don't kill time, put more life into it!'

For the welcome they extended and the unstinting help they gave, I offer sincere thanks to the following: Pham Ngoc Thack, Minister of Public Health; Colonel Ha Van Lau, official in charge of the CECAV; Ngo Dien, chief press officer at the Ministry of Foreign Affairs; Tran Huy Lieu, director of the History Institute; Ngo Duc Mau, assistant general secretary of the Union of Journalists; Nguyen Si Truc, deputy head of Xunhasaba; Tran Viet Chau, also of Xunhasaba; Hoang Trung Thong, senior official of the Writers' Union; Te Hanh and Che Lan Vien, of the Writers' Union; Phan Gia Ben, secretary of the National Committee of Vietnamese Historians; Vu Trong Kinh, official dealing with the western nations at the Committee for Cultural Relations; Vu Kuoc Thanh, head of the reception bureau at the Committee for Overseas Cultural Relations; Nguyen Phu Cuong, of the *Vietnamese Studies* team; Ngo Minh, journalist; Nguyen Dung, of the Committee for Cultural Relations.

Lastly, I wish to record my particular gratitude to Nguyen Khac Vien, editor of *Vietnamese Studies*, who was good enough to act as my guide in the early stages of my mission.

Introduction

The basic social structure in Vietnam is the village commune. This body has been in existence ever since the country became a national entity, and nowhere has it been more prominent than in the Red River delta. Flanked with pools and hedged about with stout bamboos, the Vietnamese village forms a whole and enjoys a large measure of autonomy. At one time, the state used to levy taxes and raise armies for war, yet it never set foot inside the village; it had no direct knowledge of families or individuals. When the state had obligations to meet, it demanded a given total from each village and did not concern itself with smaller details. It was the community, through its council of elders, which selected the conscripts and determined how much each household should pay. The commune was a self-administering religious and social group with sole responsibility for settling any differences which might arise between its members. Thus the state dealt, not with subjects but with communes. Expanses of common land played an important part in the life of the village and somehow managed to survive across the centuries[1].

Among the items for which the state bears responsibility is hydraulic engineering, a matter of vital importance in the Red River delta, that cradle of the Vietnamese nation. The silt in the delta was deposited there by the Red River, and from the earliest days of human habitation the river has had to be dammed as a first step towards reclaiming the land. Throughout history, damming (far more important than drainage or irrigation) has been the constant concern of state and com-

1. According to the 1931 survey, they covered about 900 square miles of the 5,800 square miles contained within the Delta. See *Les paysans du Delta Tonkinois* by P. Gourou, Paris, 1936.

munes alike, for the floods affecting the river from June to October frequently ruined what were known as the 'fifth-month' crops. The reclaiming of land within the delta probably lies at the root of the Vietnamese community, in so far as collective efforts have always been needed to dam the river. But only the state was capable of organizing hydraulic engineering on a large scale, and to this extent state and commune cannot be considered in isolation from each other: left to its own devices, the commune would not have survived.

In the first millennium B.C. the delta was inhabited by a confederation of tribes under a single leader: 'Hung' (the Hung kings). In the third century B.C. the citadel of Coloa – about twelve miles north-east of Hanoi – became the first attested capital of a properly constituted state, with its own fleet and army. The ruler was King An Zuong, of the Thuc dynasty. At about this time an event of the utmost importance to the future history of Vietnam occurred: the conquest of Bac Bo (Tonkin) by the Chinese. It led to the establishment of a centralized, bureaucratic administration run by mandarins. The commune survived, though under the mandarin system large estates were made over to the Chinese and to former tribal chieftains who had become collaborators.

Chinese domination continued for more than a thousand years, with occasional revolts – like the one staged by the Trung sisters in the first century. But all attempts to throw off the Chinese yoke proved unsuccessful until the tenth century A.D., when the struggle was taken up by the great estate-holders, of Chinese as well as Vietnamese descent. The sense of national identity – deriving from the need to reclaim the delta lands, from the cohesiveness of the communal organization, from the inherited language, and from a highly developed bronze-age civilization (brought to light by recent excavations) – had been strong enough for the Vietnamese people to absorb what the Chinese had to offer without forfeiting their own identity.

And the Chinese had plenty to offer. In the institutional

sphere: the monarchy, the mandarin bureaucracy, the introduction of large estates. In the religious and philosophical
sphere: first Buddhism, in the second century; then Confucianism; and finally, on a smaller scale, Taoism. In the
technical sphere: the widespread use of iron and paper, and –
as in Japan and Korea – the introduction of ideograms,
together with a cultural vocabulary.

In the tenth century, Vietnam was restored to independence
and went through a brief period of anarchic disintegration
under a dozen local rulers. Then, in the eleventh, twelfth and
thirteenth centuries, came the first great Vietnamese dynasty –
the Ly dynasty. The king was surrounded by an aristocracy of
dignitaries, relatives of the royal family or companions of the
line's founder. These dignitaries enjoyed the revenues of
estates bestowed by the king. Such estates were not fiefs,
however; they were apanages and remained dependencies of
the king, who was not a suzerain but a sovereign. So one
cannot talk of 'feudalism' in Vietnam. The great hydraulic
undertakings continued, the Lys transferred their capital to
Hanoi, and competitive examinations were introduced as a
method of selecting new mandarins.

The faith practised by the ruling class at this time was
orthodox Buddhism, based on renunciation and the trans-
migration of souls, and postulating the ideal of Nirvana; the
leading dignitaries were military leaders, while the civil councillors were monks – the Buddhist monasteries were surrounded by large estates. But the idea of recruiting mandarins
by competition stemmed from Confucianism, the administrative doctrine. Defence against the Chinese empire was of
fundamental importance in those days; so there was a substantial army, with a rotating roll of soldier-peasants. This same
concern with defence was the basic motive for the armed
annexation of the highland territories, the idea being that they
should absorb the initial shock of any attack. There were other

motives, too: the monarchy needed metals for making weapons and minting coins, while the people of the delta needed the bamboo and timber which the mountain regions could provide[2].

It would seem that the peasantry was divided into three categories at this time: those who worked the land on the estates, those who were domestic slaves, and those who possessed some land of their own – for private appropriation had begun.

A degree of national unity began to emerge in the early days of the Ly dynasty, with its new forms of administration. The status of the landowning peasants rose gradually but perceptibly. There was conflict between the mandarins, relegated to minor administrative duties, and the high dignitaries, who felt that their preserves were being trespassed upon. There was likewise conflict between the Buddhist councillors and the Confucian administrators and scholars[3]. In the thirteenth and fourteenth centuries, the new Tran dynasty followed more or less the same social patterns. But the struggles between the Confucians and the Buddhists intensified. The Crown showed an increasing tendency to rely on a bureaucracy of civil servants rather than on the dignitaries; for the fate of the mandarin lay in the king's hands, whereas the dignitary enjoyed a greater measure of independence. In the thirteenth century came the Mongol invasion (1280–88), ending in victory for Vietnam after a campaign combining classical and guerrilla warfare. The fourteenth was marked by an internal crisis, with large-scale peasant revolts. The Crown took steps to limit the authority of the great estates: restrictions were placed on their

2. Antagonism between the highlanders and the Kinhs (or Viets) remained rife until the war against the French. From first to last, the latter clung to the idea that the minorities would collaborate with them. They were finally proved wrong at Dien Bien Phu. The slow, patient political work of the Vietminh had prevailed over inherited bitterness.

3. See 'Marxisme et Confucianisme' by Nguyen Khac Vien, *La Pensée*, 1962.

size and on the number of household slaves employed by their owners. But the social crisis turned into a dynastic crisis, and in the end the Trans lost control.

China, now ruled by the Ming dynasty, exploited this crisis by attempting to subjugate Vietnam. The Mings controlled the country for about twenty years. They endeavoured to impose Chinese customs, seized books and deported the leading intellectuals[4]. But they met with very keen resistance. On this occasion it was led, not by the weakened monarchy, nor by the dignitaries (as at the time of the Mongol invasion), but by a peasant landowner, Le Loi, and his political adviser, a Confucian scholar who also happened to be a strategist of genius: Nguyen Trai[5]. This was a great moment in the history of Vietnam. The Chinese armies were annihilated, and the nation recovered its independence after nominally recognizing Chinese overlordship.

The establishment of the Le dynasty was a turning point in the country's affairs. The great estates disappeared almost entirely; the monarchy was stable as never before; the mandarin bureaucracy strengthened its hold; the commune flourished; most of the national territory consisted of common lands (a state of affairs which continued at least as late as the seventeenth century). Nevertheless, the landowning class tended to grow in strength and significance; it was the mainstay of the monarchy. This was the era of Confucian ideology. Society was constructed on clear, classical lines. At the apex was the king, the Son of Heaven, ruling by divine mandate. Under the king were the mandarins, often scions of landowning peasants; their posts were not hereditary. Then came the village elders, elected primarily on the basis of age. The peasants were subdivided into landowning peasants and propertyless peasants.

4. The architect who built the Mings' Imperial City in Peking was a Vietnamese: Nguyen An.
5. Nguyen Trai devised a highly original brand of politico-military guerrilla warfare. His writings have greatly influenced the leading Vietnamese strategists of the present day.

Further lands were reclaimed in the delta, and by the end of the fifteenth century the Vietnamese were striking southwards against the kingdom of Champa, in a mood of colonialist expansion.

CHARACTERISTICS OF THE VIETNAMESE COMMUNE

There used to be a saying, 'Royal edicts take second place to village rules.' And it is true that commune democracy invested the Vietnamese village with a substantial measure of autonomy and cohesion. But once the private appropriation of land began in the fifteenth century, central government under the Crown proved to have a liberating aspect: to some extent it shielded the peasants from the highhandedness of the elders as earlier, under the Ly dynasty, the Crown had protected the commune from the dignitaries. Then the central government had forbidden the seizure of common lands, which meant a great deal to the villagers, and these survived until the country finally established its independence.

The commune formed a coherent whole and was quite capable of conducting its social life without reference to the outside world. This emphasis on decentralization and division into communal units served as a barrier to the formation of extra-communal groups: guilds, castes, etc. Hence, no doubt, the failure to develop regional or provincial bodies in old Vietnam. The commune channelled every ounce of the villagers' energies into the immediate social structure. There was powerful popular belief in the existence of local genii; consequently, every village had a guardian spirit which could be prevailed upon to keep natural disasters at bay. The members of the village council were chosen from among the oldest inhabitants[6].

6. It is worth noting that this gerontocratic system differs from the family system, in which order of precedence is based on degree of kinship. The commune is no mere association of families (still less a

Once the communal system reached its fullest stage of development (round about the fifteenth century), those villages which had not yet acquired a guardian spirit proceeded to adopt one: sometimes it would be a national hero. The council of elders determined the whole range of issues relating to the life of the village: it was they who settled legal disputes, allotted vacant pieces of land and organized resistance to the elements. The house or temple (Dinh) erected in honour of the guardian spirit was also the local administrative centre, where the elders conferred, collected taxes and dispensed justice. And it was here, too, that the villagers congregated at times of celebration. Belief in the divine right of kings made Vietnamese monarchs regard themselves as heaven's representatives on earth; they even claimed precedence over the guardian spirits dwelling within their realm. Yet they were unable to enforce the appointment of village chieftains of their own choice. The communes continued to be run by elders – and in the eighteenth century they won total freedom from the central authority.

Relations within the commune were marked by a truly remarkable sense of solidarity; they were rooted in the sense of magic and religion which had built up around the guardian spirit. Contributions towards the upkeep of this form of worship were incumbent on all, for it was to the advantage of every member of the community that the village should remain in the spirit's good graces. Further, every individual was accountable to his fellows for his standards of behaviour. If one of the inhabitants scored a social success, the whole village rejoiced and took pride in the event; on the other hand, a reprehensible act by someone brought shame on the entire community. Hence the custom of making public atonement.

---

clan); if it were, the right to determine local issues would automatically belong to the assembled heads of families, as in pre-revolutionary China. The gerontocratic system likewise differs from the feudal system, which is based on the handing-down of authority.

But solidarity did not end there: it was displayed in economic terms, too. The common lands were the property of all villagers: any inhabitant who was of age was entitled to a plot[7], and in practice these common lands were cultivated just as painstakingly as privately owned acres; similarly, the communal paddy-fields were shared out every so often. Finally, there was a collective responsibility to the state for raising taxes, recruiting troops and punishing misdemeanours; from this stemmed the right of neighbours to keep close watch on one another. Within the commune, public opinion exercised absolute control over the private lives of individuals. As a result, seditious acts could not be hushed up without the collusion of the entire community. This capacity for keeping a secret was to be demonstrated time and again during the war against the French, when political cadres working for the Vietminh hid in villages for years at a time without being informed on.

Collective action endowed the villagers with a remarkable degree of security against natural – or supernatural – risks. Political threats or economic catastrophes could now be countered with acts of joint defence or mutual assistance. The successful, close-knit workings of the commune encouraged it to be jealous of its independence. For a long time, this determination to be independent helped to insulate the commune against any disruptive or innovatory influences from the outside world. The habit of communal living has made a really deep impression on the Vietnamese mentality. All expert commentators on the country's affairs have been struck by the concern with precedence displayed in the traditional Vietnamese village[8]. The peasant belonged to a hierarchy in which

7. The Vietnamese is first and foremost a farmer. Unlike the Chinese, he is seldom inclined to set up as a trader. Similarly, handicrafts used to be regarded as no more than a profitable sideline.

8. It is even possible that this characteristic helped to foster the officialism and authoritarianism of the Democratic Republic, denounced by the Party leadership in April 1967.

he was able to rise stage by stage as he grew older. By the eighteenth century, age had ceased to be the sole criterion: wealth began to play a part. One of the villager's main ambitions was to hold an honourable post within the communal household. There used to be an adage: 'Better a morsel eaten before all the assembled villagers than a hamperful eaten on one's own.' The villagers strove to achieve an honourable position which would enable them to play a useful role in the life of the community. The enclosed nature of communal society entailed a strict observance of the rules of precedence, and this was one of the things which kept the peasant from setting up home elsewhere. Outside his native village, he would have been confined to a lowlier position; indeed, he would not have succeeded in gaining a footing at all.

Moreover, there were specific economic advantages to acquiring rank within the commune. For it was the elders who determined the level of the taxes and shared out the communal paddy-fields; it was they, too, who organized the religious festivals – invariably accompanied by banquets, at which the elders regaled themselves at the community's expense. Not until the eighteenth century did the elders replace the mandarins as distributors and assessors: previously, this had been the last remaining link between state and commune. In the event, the elders very often abused their authority at the expense of ordinary inhabitants. They extorted money from their fellows and arrogated special privileges. In consequence, every member of the commune did his best to become an elder – if only to defend himself from the excesses of existing elders.

The peasant could become an elder by co-option, by election, or else, in the last resort, by sheer weight of years.

The elders' abuses were endured by the peasants because the latter were not without hope that they too might be elders one day. The democratic denial of hereditary rights and the provision of universal opportunities for promotion (if only with the coming of old age) invested the commune with a certain stability.

All these factors combined to strengthen the Vietnamese peasant's attachment to the village in which he was born. Mention must also be made of the cardinal fact that his ancestors were buried there; he would have felt it entirely unseemly to worship them on someone else's land. Indeed, the old scholars always depicted the lot of the homeless vagabond as the most wretched that could befall any human being.

At the end of the sixteenth century, the Le dynasty entered a period of crisis which deepened in the seventeenth. The common lands, which the Crown wished to preserve as a safeguard against peasant revolts, were encroached on by the landowning class (of which the elders were members). Confucianism lost its prestige, and the Confucianists split into two camps: some continued to support the hierarchy, the king and the mandarins, while others – scholars who had failed to qualify for the mandarinate by competitive examination – lived side by side with the ordinary peasants in the villages, espousing their cause and often acting as their leaders. The crisis spread to the court – where the Les continued as nominal heads of state, though the real power was now exercised by a family of dignitaries, the Trinhs, and by the military commanders. This situation – a compound of social, dynastic and philosophical crises – finally exploded in the eighteenth century, when it was doubtless triggered off by the demographic crisis.

For, despite the Vietnamese peasant's extreme attachment to his village, the need for more land made it necessary for the nation to expand southwards. This process continued from the eleventh century to the eighteenth, a period of nearly eight hundred years. It was no sudden, sweeping act of colonization but a slow, arduous clearing of the areas beyond the existing borders. The settlers were the inhabitants of villages lying quite close to the land which needed to be brought into cultivation. A given village would establish a new hamlet within easy reach, for the settlers had no desire to break with their native commune; they wanted to be free to return there at any time. The connexions between the two endured for years and were only severed when the hamlet broke away by asking to be listed as a separate community within the state[9]. Another form of colonization encouraged by the central government was the clearing of areas in Nam Bo by parties of ex-convicts.

The Vietnamese settlers moved into unoccupied areas, but as soon as the soil became fertile the Cham authorities asserted their right to it. The conflicts which inevitably ensued led to armed intervention by the Vietnamese kings, and these periodic wars resulted in the annexation of further territory. The setting-up of military bases drove the Chams or the Cambodians even farther back within their own borders.

This territorial expansion was the necessary concomitant of a growing population. So long as such expansion was possible, a balance could be maintained. The kingdom of Champa was finally eliminated in the seventeenth century.

At the end of that century[10], and in the course of the eighteenth, the balance tilted sharply in favour of the newly

9. At the present time, tens of thousands of peasants are being transferred from the delta to open up new areas in the highlands. I was able to observe for myself how closely these peasants keep in touch with their native communes, financially and in other ways. There is scope for some fascinating research into the way new co-operatives are set up and incorporated into the framework of existing national minorities.

10. It was in the seventeenth century that the French Jesuits came to Vietnam, following the example set by the Portuguese in the sixteenth, and by the British and Dutch. These Jesuits – and above all the Foreign Missions Society – became firmly established in the country and taught the two royal families, the Tranhs in the north and the Nguyens in the south, to cast cannons as a way of coming to terms with each other.

conquered regions in the south (i.e. the Mekong delta). These regions were rich in agricultural potentialities, and a long way removed from the harsh conditions prevailing in Bac Bo. Conscious of their wealth, they tried to break away from the rest of the kingdom. The likelihood of a split was intensified by the economic decentralization inherent in the communal system. Vietnam was 1,250 miles long and had grown too big for the existing methods of administration. Another family, the Nguyens, still nominally subordinate to the Les, assumed power south of the eighteenth parallel and then seceded. The rise in population produced a degree of overcrowding in the eighteenth century which would certainly seem to have been the major cause of the violent social crises which shook Vietnam.

Thus the eighteenth century was a time of large-scale peasant risings, which threatened the monarchy and proved extremely hard to put down. Most of these risings were led by eminent Confucian scholars (who quoted Mancius's 'right to rebel')[11]. About 1770 came the massive Tay Son revolt in central Annam (Trung Bo). This swept the Nguyens from their position of authority in the south and then spread northwards, inflicting defeat on the Trinhs and keeping the Les on the throne. The Nguyens secured the support of the Siamese; but the latter were beaten by Nguyen Hue, another outstanding strategist. In the north, the Les sought assistance from the Manchu dynasty (the Quings), who occupied Hanoi but were eventually defeated by Nguyen Hue at the battle of Dong Da (1789).

The Le dynasty was driven from the throne. Various reforms followed: the common lands were redistributed and the displaced peasants re-absorbed; in the cultural sphere, the national tongue was adopted as the official language – a change which marked the end of court Chinese.

11. In addition, a discernible Buddhist revival began in the seventeenth century.

But the Tay Son interlude was short-lived. After a period of exile in Siam, the Nguyens succeeded in driving the Tay Sons out[12]. The establishment of the Nguyen dynasty in 1802 – these were the ancestors of Bao Dai – restored the state's authority. The code observed by the Les, which had owed its inspiration to national customs, was replaced by a mere copy of the code instituted by the Quings (including, for example, no rights for women). The ensuing period was marked by a return to scholastic orthodoxy and to a traditionalist administration run by mandarins who had achieved office through success in competitive examinations. Before long, concessions were being made to France, and in 1858 the French conquest began – in the south (Cochin China). A peace treaty, under which certain territories were handed over, was violated by the occupying power. The court foundered, and total annexation followed (1884).

The distinctive qualities of the Vietnamese national character had been moulded by the way of life prevailing in the villages, with their entirely communal basis, their relative independence and their peculiar solidarity. The continual need to build dikes and dams – without them, there could be no paddy-fields – had fostered the ingeniousness and capacity for taking pains which were high among the virtues of the peasants living in the delta. Finally, the frequent invasions by the Chinese, the Mongols and others, and the resistance with which these had been met, had developed excellent fighting qualities in the Vietnamese people; so had their own steady expansion towards the Mekong delta.

This accounts for the sustained resistance which the scholar-

12. The Nguyens asked the apostolic vicar of the Cochin China Mission (i.e. the area headquarters of the Jesuit Foreign Missions) for help in overthrowing the Tay Sons, and French troops from India played a part in restoring them to power. For further information about this period, see Christiane Rageau's thesis *Gia-Long et les Européens*, Paris, 1968.

patriots were able to mount against the French between 1860 and the early years of the twentieth century (the last guerrilla stronghold was not subdued until 1913). The scholars were either retired mandarins or men who, after failing to qualify in the competitive examinations, had chosen to live and teach in the villages.

Even before the Scholars' Revolt began, two wholly peasant-inspired insurrections broke out in the southern province of Long An (otherwise known as Tan An): one, lasting from 1860 until 1864, was led by Truong Dinh, the other by Nguyen Van Lich.

The Scholars' Revolt took place chiefly in the north of Trung Bo (old Annam) and – to a lesser extent – in the delta. There were four major insurrections: the Ba Dinh rising (1886–91) in the province of Thanh Hoa; the Bai Say rising (1885–9) on the borders of the provinces of Hung Yen and Hai Duong; the Hung Linh rising (1886–92) in the province of Thanh Hoa; and finally the Huong Khe rising (1886–96) which spread to four provinces (Ha Tinh, Thanh Hoa, Nghe An and Quang Binh).

These peasant risings were extremely interesting. The rebels employed guerrilla tactics, harrying the colonial army and carefully avoiding pitched battles. Vast subterranean galleries were dug beneath the villages, so that the defenders could hold out against siege, and in general a remarkable capacity was shown for lengthy resistance based entirely on the use of local forces, without support from the state. The part which secret societies played during this period was far from negligible[13].

The last substantial rising was led by a peasant, De Tham, at Yen The in the province of Ha Bac. His followers had been stripped of their lands as a result of the concessions made to the French settlers in Tonkin. This insurrection continued

13. cf. Chesneaux, *Les Sociétés secrètes en Chine*, Julliard, *Archives*, 1966. A chapter is devoted to Vietnam.

from 1887 until 1913, and even then it was crushed only after a thorough combing of the entire province.

The Scholars' Revolt had several weaknesses. It did not jell as a nation-wide movement. It had no political programme, except to restore a monarchy which refused to capitulate. Finally, it had no clearly defined policy *vis-à-vis* the minorities[14]; and so it inevitably foundered once it was driven back into the highlands.

France did not begin to invest seriously in Vietnam until the early years of the twentieth century. And it was only after the First World War that colonial society emerged in its fully fledged state. Hitherto the colonial administration had worked hand in glove with the existing administrative apparatus: king, mandarins, elders. Before long, however, new social classes began to emerge, brought into being by the introduction of city life and a capitalist economy: the proletariat which provided the manpower for the mines, the rubber plantations, the railways, etc.; the merchants; the bourgeoisie (a rickety group, this); and, most significant of all, the petty bourgeoisie, consisting of minor civil servants and semi-intellectuals. The peasantry was ruined by a monetary economy which required them to pay taxes in hard cash, while the artisans suffered a significant decline. The colonial regime bled the countryside of its resources without making any contribution in return. More and more land fell into fewer and fewer hands: in the Mekong delta, a new class of great landowners was born.

Between the turn of the century and the creation of the Indochinese Communist Party (1930), there were many and varied displays of national feeling; but they were never sufficiently well organized to challenge the colonial regime in a comprehensive manner.

Until the First World War, the scholars followed the

14. For instance, the French made effective use of Catholic elements among the Vietnamese; but the scholars were hostile to them, insisting on the need to rid the country of this 'foreign heresy'.

example set by the Japanese: the Dong Du movement was formed from the officially authorized bodies (very often linked with the secret societies) which sprang up in the cities – e.g. the Dong Kinh Nghia Thuc (Private Institution of Tonkin) and the Vietnam Quang Phuc Hoi (Association for the Restoration of Vietnam). In Nam Bo (Cochin China), millennialist-type movements began to emerge: the Thien Dia Hoi (Heaven and Earth Association) and others, frequently retrograde in ideology. Revolts flared up, such as the one staged by the Thai Nguyens in 1917–18.

After the First World War, the petty bourgeoisie took over from the scholars. They drew their inspiration from the liberal ideology of parliamentary democracy. They had no land reform programme, but were keen to promote industrialization and modernization. The various parties which came into being at this time were 'anti-feudal', but in a cultural rather than an economic sense. It was at this point that the Cao Dai movement was born. The influence of Sun Yat-sen's ideas was very strong, and the most substantial movement of the time was the Vietnam Quoc Dan Dang, closely modelled on the Kuomintang. It enjoyed fairly widespread support but was shorn of its leadership in 1930 after organizing a military mutiny at Yen Bay. A few prominent members managed to escape the severe repression which followed, and fled to China. In February of the same year, the Vietnamese Communist Party was formed, deriving its nucleus from the Thanh Nien – the revolutionary youth movement which Ho Chi Minh had established five years earlier, at the time of the great university strikes of 1925–6. Nine months later, the new party changed its name to the Indochinese Communist Party.

Marxism had been brought into Vietnam along two routes: (a) from France, through Communist seamen docking at Saigon and Haiphong, and (b) from China. The outstanding characteristic of the Vietnamese Marxist movement was that it embraced and absorbed the existing nationalist elements. As yet, no comprehensive history has been published of the Indochinese Communist Party, or Vietnamese Workers' Party as it afterwards became; but a brief summary may be useful. In the days of the revolutionary youth movement, the nucleus of the future party was made up of petty-bourgeois and semi-intellectuals; a number of young people were sent to Canton, in China, to be trained by Ho Chi Minh, while the general instruction was for as many members as possible to obtain jobs in various industrial concerns (the mines, rubber plantations, and so on employed about 220,000 workers in 1930). The 1929 crisis brought much quicker and harsher consequences in Vietnam than in France. There were industrial strikes, and the peasantry began to stir for the first time since the turn of the century. 1931 was the year of the 'Nghe Tinh Soviets'[15], an insurrectionary movement launched by poor and middling, rather than landless, peasants. The Party was doing its best to establish itself in the rural areas. The rising lasted three months and was then crushed with extreme severity. Thousands of people, including a great many militants, were sent to the island penal colony of Poulo Condore.

The first programme drawn up by the Party, in February 1930, provided for land distribution and the confiscation of church property, but made no mention of agrarian reform in favour of the landless peasants, who were regarded as workers. This mistake was put right three months later.

The years 1931–4 were marked by a wave of repression which successfully re-established colonial law and order. The Party Secretary, Tran Phu, was arrested and tortured to death. At that time, Ho Chi Minh was the Comintern's representative in South-east Asia, operating now in China, now in Siam. The Communists worked hand in hand with the Trotskyites, especially in Nam Bo; the two groups even ran a joint newspaper in Saigon. In 1934 the Party started putting down roots

15. *The Soviets of Nghe-Tinh* by Tran Huy Lieu, Foreign Languages Publishing House, Hanoi, 1960.

again, and two years later it operated openly and lawfully, on a fairly broad scale, under the more liberal colonial administration which came into being after the formation of the Popular Front government in Paris. The Popular Front line adopted by the Third International had considerable repercussions in Vietnam. Demands for national independence were dropped in favour of an alliance with the bourgeoisie. It was decided that the Party should co-operate with the colonial government in the war against fascism. Finally, the Trotskyites – who for half a dozen years had stood together with the Communists against all the election candidates put up by the colonial regime in the southern part of the country – were now liquidated.

The Party made preparations which would allow it to function on two levels: the open and the clandestine. On the surface, tolerated by the regime, were newspapers and political rallies pressing for such democratic reforms as the eight-hour day, freedom of association, freedom to strike, freedom to travel as one pleased within the country's borders. A considerable number of detainees were released from Poulo Condore (including Pham Van Dong). Soon, however, the fall of the Popular Front government in France brought a new wave of repression in Vietnam. The Democratic Front of 1936 was replaced by a united, anti-imperialist National Front. And there was a change in the Party's slogans *vis-à-vis* the peasantry. In 1936 there had merely been talk of redistributing the common lands, but in 1939 it was further stated that property held by unpatriotic landowners and tenant farmers would be confiscated and nationalized (attacks on excessive rents and interest rates continued).

The repression grew worse with the outbreak of the Second World War, and the Party went completely underground.

At the seventh session of the Central Committee, in October 1940, there was another slight modification in the Party's attitude to the peasantry. The following decisions were taken:

1. All property in the hands of landowners, the church and unpatriotic organizations or individuals was to be nationalized.

2. Rents and perquisites (gifts to elders, etc.) were to be cut.

3. Confiscated lands were to be nationalized and shared out among the needier peasants and the revolutionary militants.

Not long afterwards, the Japanese invaded the country. Their occupation was purely strategic and economic, and they made no attempt to dismantle the existing colonial administration. So the Vietnamese now had to live under a double yoke. Much of the rice crop was sent to Japan, and living standards sank lower than ever – especially since the European colony, denied imports from Europe, began to draw far more heavily on the country's resources.

At the eighth session of the Central Committee in May 1941 – the most important of the sessions held before the August revolution – the role attributed to the peasants was accentuated. Until then, the Vietnamese leaders had taken the view that the cities must inevitably be the starting point for an insurrection. But now the Central Committee decided that there was no more urgent task than securing national liberation: in consequence, the worker-peasant alliance must be strengthened and the Party's peasant basis consolidated, with due consideration for the highland minorities. In this period, the Party's strongest bases were the provinces bordering on China: Cao Bang, Lang Son, Bac Can and – north of Hanoi – Thai Nguyen. In 1941 the Vietminh National Front was formed: the first resistance base was established in Viet Bac, a highland region inhabited by minorities, not far from the Chinese frontier. Slowly but surely, the Vietminh Front set up committees all over the country, encouraging the peasants to make a stand against the Franco-Japanese rice requisitions and the compulsory growing of jute introduced by the occupying power. The cadres moved into the villages, initially concentrating on the highland areas, which were of vital strategic importance and where colonial rule was less well established. The power of the Vietminh gradually spread. On 9 March 1945 the Japanese did away with the French administration and set up the Bao Dai government. The Vietminh proceeded to confiscate settlers' estates wherever it could. In addition, it combated the severe famine by seizing stocks of rice held by the Japanese and sharing them out among the peasants; this was in August 1945, when Japan was about to capitulate. Clearly the moment was ripe for the long-awaited nation-wide insurrection. Throughout the country, military activity was supported by mass demonstrations. The uprising gained a hold in Nam Bo before the authorities had a chance to re-establish order. The rebels seized power on a local basis, setting up a People's Administrative Committee in each district. Hanoi was captured on 19 August. On 2 September 1945, the Democratic Republic of Vietnam was proclaimed. The settlers' estates were shared out. But land reform measures against Vietnamese owners were not embarked on until March 1953. The Party merely launched a campaign to reduce rents.

There is no need to dwell on this period[16], during which a temporary British occupation allowed the French to reassert themselves in the south while Chiang Kai-shek moved into the north. The outcome of the negotiations leading to the agreements of 6 March 1946 is well known. The first Indochinese war began in December 1946 and lasted over seven years. Bernard Fall, in his *Last Reflections*, emphasizes the fact that the Vietminh had chosen to clash militarily with a French government which *enjoyed Communist backing*.

Not until December 1953 did the land reform programme begin to operate in earnest, after a period of mass mobilization in the liberated zone carried out by cadres who had dwelt side by side with the poor peasants, practising the 'three

16. See *Histoire du Vietnam de 1940 à 1952* by Philippe Devillers, Editions du Seuil, Paris, 1952.

togethers': living together, eating together, working together. Elders and landowners were publicly arraigned in an effort to discredit them. Already, ultra-leftist errors were being perpetrated – errors which could only repel many of the people whose support was being canvassed. And yet the overall results, though not outstanding, seem to have gone a long way towards turning Dien Bien Phu into a victory for land reform. The battle was fought 250 miles away from the delta, and but for the mobilization of peasants on a really huge scale the Vietnamese forces could never have been provisioned. The Vietnamese had realized from the first that Dien Bien Phu would be the culmination of the winter 1953–spring 1954 campaign.

General

The Democratic Republic of Vietnam covers an area of 63,000 square miles and has about eighteen million inhabitants[17]. It is subject to monsoons: the north-east monsoon from November to April, the south-west monsoon from May to October. There is an average rainfall of sixty inches in the plains and ninety inches in the highlands.

Away from the coastal area, the country may be divided into three regions:

1. The highlands, amounting to two thirds of the national territory. Densely wooded, these areas contain only a fifth of the country's population and a mere 5 per cent of its arable land.

2. The middle regions include broad tracts of land which might be brought into cultivation; but a number of denuded hills have suffered erosion and are now being retimbered.

3. The Red River delta, the storehouse of North Vietnam, containing 74 per cent of the arable land and 75 per cent of the population.

The Red River has a total length of 750 miles, but only 300 miles of it flow through Vietnam. Its delta covers a mere 6,000 square miles – a triangle with Phu Tho as its apex. The alluvial deposits at the mouth of the river choke the land lying close to the sea, which recedes at a rate of about a hundred yards a year. The density of population is approximately 350 inhabitants per square mile; in places it even rises above 400 – whereas in the highlands the figure varies between four and twenty.

17. Between 85 and 88 per cent of these are Kinhs (or Viets). The rest are made up of national minorities such as the Thais, the Meos, etc.

The Structure of Vietnam

THE STATE

1. A central government elected by a National Assembly which meets every two years. The National Assembly has a standing committee and a number of other committees.

An election for membership of the National Assembly is held every four years (the latest was in 1964).

2. The Provinces.

The Administrative Committee of each province is elected by a provincial People's Council.

3. The district (approximately 400 districts, with twenty or thirty villages per district).

There is a District Committee, elected by the representatives of the Communes.

4. The Communes.

These are managed by People's Councils (elected by general vote) and an Administrative Committee (elected by the People's Councils).

THE PARTY

1. The cells (within a co-operative, factory, etc.).

2. The branch, covering the entire commune. This elects a Party Committee for the commune. The Committee, in turn, elects its own Bureau – including a Secretary.

3. Delegates from the local branches attend a conference at district level to elect the District Committee.

4. The Provincial Committee is elected by delegates from the local branches (like the District Committee).

5. The National Congress. Here delegates from the provinces, the cities and the state enterprises elect the Central Committee.

THE NEW REGIME AND THE PEASANTS

Table 1. Redistribution of land in 1945[18].

Categories	Area (in acres)	Percentage of total area
Settlers	37,417.52	1
Church	59,626.26	1.5
Common or semi-common lands	986,437.89	25
Landowners	965,729.12	24.5
Rich peasants	279,864.39	7.1
Average peasants	1,143,107.96	29
Poor peasants	418,885.16	10
Agricultural workers	43,259.25	1.1
Other labourers	31,534.01	0.8

In the period immediately following the August 1945 revolution, 80 per cent of the Vietnamese population were peasants; of these, 61.5 per cent had no land. Despite the difficult wartime conditions, the Vietminh managed to organize the building or rebuilding of some 20 million cubic yards of dikes. Prior to 1963, various steps were taken to improve the lot of the poor and landless peasantry; but these steps were still limited in scope. Ground rents were reduced by 25 per cent in 1945, and private estates which had been left unattended were made over to the needy. In 1947, plots of state-owned land were distributed in the liberated zones, at the rate of seven and a half acres per family. In 1949–50, property belonging to settlers and Vietnamese collaborators was expropriated and shared out, on a provisional basis, among the families of fighting men. And debts contracted before August 1945 were wiped out.

In 1953 – rather late, in the view of the Vietnamese leaders themselves (for they considered that the programme should

18. Based on statistics issued by the Land Reform Committee of the Democratic Republic of Vietnam. The metric equivalents of these figures are quoted in *Le Vietnam socialiste* by Le Chau, F. Maspero, Paris, 1966.

have been set in motion two years earlier) – land reform measures were applied in the liberated territories. It was decided that 15 per cent of the cultivated land should be distributed, a ruling which affected half the villages in the present Democratic Republic.

Table 2. Land reform in the 3,035 villages of North Vietnam (in acres[19])

Nature of land distributed	August 1945- July 1949	July 1949- April 1953	Total 1945-53
Settlers'	28,802	13,153	41,955
Religious communities'	—	18,463	18,463
Common and semi-common	188,110	268,706	456,816
State	63,065	186,229	249,294
TOTAL	279,977	486,551	766,528
Percentage of total area of land held by same villages	22	37	59

In all, barely 20 per cent of the toiling peasants derived any benefit from these interim measures. But between early 1955 and June 1956, a far more sweeping land reform programme was carried out. The Vietnamese peasantry was classified under the following headings:

1. Landless peasants.

2. Poor peasants. These did not have a large enough plot to provide a living for their families and were obliged to rent other land or let their own.

3. Average peasants. These owned enough land to provide for their families' needs.

4. Rich peasants. These worked their own land and hired additional labour.

5. Landowners. The greater part of their income derived from the exploitation of other people's labour (especially through rent and usury).

19. Statistics issued by the Land Reform Committee of the D R V.

The land reform programme was implemented by the Party cadres – the Can Bos. 'Offenders' were subjected to public arraignment, in the belief that such occasions would cause what Nguyen Khac Vien described as a 'collective emotional shock'.

Table 3. Average endowment of land per head before and after the land reform programme (in square yards[20])

Types of producers	Before	After
Landowners	8,108	986
Rich peasants	2,531	2,582
Average peasants	1,195	1,872
Poor peasants	410	1,641
Hired peasants	—	1,700

This time the land reform programme extended to 65 per cent of the arable land. Two hundred thousand acres, 107,000 draught animals and 1,846,000 farming implements were shared out among 2,200,000 peasant families consisting of nine million persons – i.e. 72 per cent of the rural population. By the time the programme was concluded, the total area of cultivated lands was 24 per cent (one million acres) higher than in 1939. Yield per acre had risen by 36 per cent, overall production by 68.4 per cent, production per head by nearly 43 per cent (i.e. 46 lb.) and individual consumption by 13.5 per cent (57 lb.).

But the programme was pushed through in a mechanical, leftist manner which frequently led to mistakes and which claimed a good many victims. In September 1956, the Vietnamese cabinet met to consider reports of abuses. The special privileges accorded to the Land Reform Committees were withdrawn and the special People's Tribunals abolished. Two months later, a peasants' revolt broke out in the province of Nghe An, but this was swiftly crushed.

20. Nguyen Xuan Lai, quoted by Le Chau, op. cit.

According to the Workers' Party newspaper, *Nhan Dan*[21], 30 per cent of the peasants convicted as landowners were not really landowners at all. The Can Bos had determinedly set out to find a given percentage of landowners per village. Admittedly, the pattern of ownership in Vietnam, and especially in the Red River delta, did not make the task an easy one.

The principal landowners were not eager to betray their identity; indeed, they tended to conceal their wealth, especially if they were former or practising mandarins. The habit was widespread, for nothing could be simpler than to accuse them of lining their pockets by abusing their administrative powers. But it would be hard to gauge the extent of their possessions if these were dotted about in several villages and officially credited to various relatives[22].

The errors marring the execution of the land reform programme were examined by the tenth session of the Workers' Party Central Committee in September 1956. One result was the replacement of Truong Chinh as party secretary. The errors varied from village to village, but were generally ascribable to two basic political blunders:

1. The criteria defining the various social categories had not been adhered to. So rich peasants had been looked upon as landowners, and average peasants as rich peasants; even poor peasants had been subjected to attacks. Patriotic landowners had been treated as collaborationist landowners.

2. Freedom of religious conscience had been gravely violated in traditionally Catholic areas, and the strict terms of the programme had been unimaginatively applied in zones inhabited by national minorities.

The mistakes in the programme (which had been modelled on the Chinese land reform measures) were corrected as far as possible, village by village, between September 1956 and

21. Issue dated 13 August 1967.
22. P. Gourou, op. cit.

March 1958. During this time, productivity rose swiftly, with the result that the output figures for 1957 were twice those of 1955.

After a temporary setback, mutual aid began again: several families would club together at harvest time and planting-out time. Land and crops were not pooled, however. Labour was remunerated at the proper rates. So this was not mutual aid in the traditional sense.

The next step was a rudimentary form of production co-operative[23].

Farming became collective: there was a system of joint management, but individuals retained ownership of their own land. The year 1959 saw the introduction of the co-operative in the strict sense of the word: according to the Party, this was a necessary aim if production was to be increased. Initially, only a few volunteers fell in with the scheme. Land and implements were pooled; private ownership was abolished and remuneration based strictly on quantity of work contributed. At the end of the first year, the co-operative peasants obtained a lower profit than those operating independently. It was a bad moment for the Party workers: they had no more experience of organizing labour than anybody else, and to make matters worse the peasants seemed to be adopting the same attitude within the co-operatives as they had shown in the old days of working for landowners. The yield was lower than among the independent workers. At that time there was a more or less free market, and some of the independent peasants began to hire others who were less astute; they then sold their rice on the open market, realizing substantial profits. Despite near-equality in terms of acreage, a new form of differentiation was emerging. Meanwhile the state – as a result of the Party's

23. *Etudes vietnamiennes*, No. 2: 'Problèmes agricoles'. See also the relevant resolutions of the fifth Plenum of the Workers' Party Central Committee (1961) and the statutes of the rudimentary farming co-operatives.

efforts – had succeeded in mobilizing the peasants and reducing, if not eliminating, the risk of floods. A scheme for damming the main channels of the Red River was financed nationally. New dams, canals and irrigation systems made it possible for rice to be grown on high ground. Finally, the low-lying areas were drained so as to limit the havoc wreaked in the rainy season. Before long, two or even three rice crops a year became a practical proposition over a wider area.

The Party persevered in its policy of collectivization, and in the second year the co-operative workers achieved the same level as the independents. Soon the former were enjoying the benefits of the improved water management, which enabled them to bring in several harvests a year, while direct assistance from the state gave the co-operatives one advantage after another. In addition, the free market was curtailed; the small landowners were no longer able to dispose of their rice or take on labour from outside the family. As a result, the co-operatives began to attract an increasing number of peasants, and in a short while there were socialist or semi-socialist co-operatives everywhere – the latter paying a ground rent to the former landowners.

Table 4. Farming co-operatives.

	1955	1956	1957	1958	1959	1960
Total	7	37	44	4,722	28,875	41,401
Percentage of peasant homes				5%	45.4%	85.8%
Advanced co-operatives					1,033	4,885
Number of families per co-operative				36	42	58

By the beginning of 1961, 85 per cent of the nation's farming had been collectivized and 10 per cent of the resulting groups were socialist co-operatives.

Agricultural production showed a continuing increase of about 4 per cent, a quite remarkable figure which impressed all observers[24].

24. René Dumont, 'Problèmes agricoles au Nord-Vietnam', published in *France-Asie* No. 183, 1965.

The co-operatives ran into a number of difficulties, especially in the fields of management, planned production and distribution of income. These difficulties were basically due to the lack of democratic administration (all decisions stemmed from above) and to the poor technical qualifications of the officials in charge.

In addition, North Vietnam sought to diversify its output, growing a greater quantity of crops (jute, cotton, sugar-cane) and going in for more fish-breeding. By 1962, collectivization and irrigation and drainage works were to all intents and purposes complete. Efforts were also made to increase the input of fertilizers by growing manure crops (azollae) and making rational use of human manure (septic tank). Farming implements were improved, too: the co-operatives were provided with ploughs for deep tilling, improved harrows, and new equipment for threshing and planting. Meanwhile the country was embarking on its first five-year plan (1961–5), which was to have laid the foundations for industrialization but had to be left unfinished because of the escalation of the war. (In 1954 there were forty-one industrial concerns in the Democratic Republic, only five of them modern; in 1964 there were 1,100, large and small alike.) The average annual growth during the period 1954–64 was 8 per cent. Just before escalation began, substantial changes were introduced in the rural areas. Standards rose; new farming techniques were perfected. Production continued to increase. A far cry from the conditions prevailing in 1945, when two million Vietnamese died of starvation.

The view is often expressed that North Vietnam has been able to stand up to the escalation of the war because it remains a backward, unindustrialized country. This is only partly true. In fact, its success in holding out is due to its high organizational and technical standards at village and provincial level. What 'underdeveloped' country can pride itself on having a school and a competently staffed medical unit in every village ?

North Vietnam can. At district level, there are second- and third-phase schools and hospitals for cases too serious to be dealt with by the village medical unit. At provincial level, there are other third-phase schools, vocational schools and hospitals where the most intricate operations can be carried out. The province is self-sufficient for the bulk of its health, educational and nutritional needs.

During the years of peace, considerable efforts were made in this sphere. For the period 1954–64 the figures were as in Table 5.

Table 5.

Number of adults who had received full first-phase education (four classes)	2,760,250[25]
Number of adults who had received full second-phase education (seven classes)	377,170
Number of adults who had received full third-phase education (ten classes)	37,245
Number of persons graduating from higher education	15,289
Number of pupils emerging from vocational schools	57,127

Table 6. Development of Education in North Vietnam.

	1955	1964-5
General education	746,000	2,666,000
Infant classes	522,500	780,000
Teaching staff		75,000
Higher education		
Teaching staff	1,200	26,300
Vocational schools	—	2,200
Number of pupils	2,800	35,600

In 1967 there were 6 per cent more pupils in North Vietnam than in 1965. All children between the ages of seven and eleven receive first-phase education. The second phase lasts three years, and so does the third. There are infant classes for children between six and seven, and nursery schools for those between three and six. Adults achieved literacy several years ago, following the Workers' Party decision to adopt the national language at all stages of instruction.

25. *Etudes vietnamiennes*, No. 6.

There has been no radical modification of these programmes, but since 1965 certain subjects have been simplified, with a greater focusing on essentials, to make up for time lost through air raids and the long and difficult journeys to school. Classrooms have been adapted to the needs of war; aisles between seats have been turned into trenches, and teachers – with the help of workers from the local co-operatives – have built shelters and defensive walls to reduce the danger from shrapnel. The pupils wear helmets of stoutly plaited straw and carry individual first-aid kits. Material difficulties (shortage of exercise books, pencils, etc.) are great, but the will to learn is even greater: the children are told they are participating in the struggle by learning more and learning better. The war is never lost sight of, even in art lessons: almost every clay model is of a military aircraft. The older and more advanced pupils receive not only general education and political training, but an introduction to agricultural science. Soil, manure, seeds, hydraulic problems, farming implements: all these are studied, with practical work on the school's experimental plot. Thus the pupils receive an education adapted to the needs of the society from which they spring, and the knowledge they acquire eventually enables them to make a contribution towards technical improvements in the rural areas. Those who do not go on to the university or to a vocational school are placed under the supervision of the technical team running the local co-operative. The teachers meet and confer with this team so that the best possible use can be made of their pupils' skills.

First-phase teachers are required to have completed seven classes in general education and spent two years at a teachers' training college; second-phase teachers, ten classes and two years at training college; third-phase, five years at training college.

Adult evening classes are held throughout the country, and these are very well attended. The particular aura which has always surrounded the scholar in Vietnam has established a long tradition of learning, and – war or no war – the state encourages it as a means of raising the nation's cultural and technological standards. Many villages also run nursery schools; and there is a smaller, but not negligible, proportion of crèches.

Health Problems

Air warfare presents a particular problem: casualties can occur anywhere, at any time. In Vietnam, where communication and transport are hampered by bombing raids, it has been decided that treatment should be available on the spot, wherever it is needed. The difficulty is that such a decision calls for an extremely decentralized medical system, a requirement altogether at odds with what is generally understood by 'underdevelopment'. The government did not wait for the escalation of the war before embarking on a system of this kind, unlike many newly-independent countries in Asia and Africa, where capital cities have been pampered at the expense of rural areas.

When the republic first gained its independence, the health service was in a deplorable condition. There was a great shortage of staff. Doctors, auxiliaries, midwives and orderlies were banded together and dispatched to the country districts. The initial effort was prophylactic in aim, prevention being better than cure. Water lay at the root of a great many diseases: given the slightest rainfall, every form of impurity got swept into the pools. So steps were taken to ensure greater cleanliness in the villages: double septic tanks were built, the rice-fields properly manured, the wells suitably covered in . . .

In 1955, there was one doctor per 150,000 inhabitants and one officer of health per 80,000; in 1965, one doctor per 8,700 inhabitants and one officer of health per 1,850[26].

In the space of a few years, widespread vaccination virtually eliminated smallpox, malaria and poliomyelitis; there are only occasional outbreaks of typhoid. To gain time, medical auxiliaries were given specialist training in those diseases which occurred most frequently in the villages. In 1959, operations

26. cf. *Etudes vietnamiennes*, No. 5.

for entropion (caused through trachoma) could be performed only in Hanoi – and there were hundreds of thousands of cases of trachoma. The auxiliaries were taught how to make incisions in the eyelid and then restitch the skin, an operation which was technically simple though calling for great care in execution. Today, trachoma has all but disappeared; on the few occasions when it does occur, it is treated at village level.

With the escalation of the war, the number of surgeons and assistant surgeons has risen sharply. Each commune has a health committee of three, four or five members, responsible for hygiene and preventing disease. And each village medical post contains a nurse and a maternity unit.

In the course of 248 raids between February 1965 and August 1967, 127 medical or health establishments were destroyed, including one Institute, twenty-four hospitals of between three and five hundred beds (out of thirty provincial hospitals in North Vietnam), thirty-nine district hospitals (i.e. 20 per cent of the total), nine specialist hospitals (each containing between two and sixteen hundred beds) and one treatment centre. Despite these blows, the country managed to train 1,367 qualified doctors and 3,408 medical auxiliaries in the course of the same three years. That raiding the sick was a deliberate policy became clear as long ago as June 1965 when the leper hospital at Quynh Lap, containing 2,000 beds, was bombed thirty-two times in forty-eight hours.

The Origins of Escalation

The Americans' decision to escalate the war stemmed from their failure to make headway in South Vietnam between 1963 and 1965. It was felt that a strategy consisting of graduated air attacks would reduce the flow of material aid from north to south, bring Hanoi to its knees and so isolate the NLF.

After the signing of the Geneva Agreements, the Diem government strove to establish its authority in South Vietnam. Within two years, American 'advisers' had filled the gap left by the French colonial troops. There was still no sign of the democratic elections which were supposed to determine the country's future. The Diem regime had set up a police state backed by the Americans and drawing most of its support from the million Catholics who had deserted from the North[27]. These developments brought the problem of South Vietnam's future to a head.

Diem proceeded to make three major errors which led to the formation of the NLF and to his own downfall:

1. As soon as independence was declared, he took away the lands which the Vietminh had handed over to the peasants (about five million acres).

2. In 1956 he stopped the villages from electing their own representatives, in clear violation of the communal tradition. Instead, he appointed village chiefs (Ac-Ons); these were soon liquidated by the guerrillas, acting with the knowledge and co-operation of the villagers.

3. He won the enmity of religious sects and national minorities alike. His extraordinarily harsh repressive measures

27. It was once remarked that the crucifixes of many members of the local Catholic hierarchy seemed to have been hewn from the same wood as truncheons.

prompted both the ex-Vietminh militants and the 'patriots' to engage in an armed struggle for survival. It was, in fact, local initiatives and *not* incitements from Hanoi which sparked off the second war of resistance, long before the NLF was formed (December 1960). The repression is reported to have claimed about 170 thousand victims between 1954 and 1959.

Meanwhile American intervention, which dates back to 27 June 1950, when Truman sent a military mission to Saigon[28], was growing all the time. The strength of US forces in the south, which stood at four thousand men in 1961, had risen to fifteen thousand by late 1963; by September 1965 the figure had swollen to 128 thousand; by the beginning of 1968, it was half a million[29].

The strategy of what was later to become the NLF may be divided into several phases:

- 1959–60. The aim was to loosen the stranglehold by demolishing the close supervision exercised over the villages.
- 1960. The peasants in the Mekong delta were urged to put a brake on the 'Special War' while guerrilla forces were built up.
- 1961–5. Now came continuous warfare against 600,000 government troops and 20,000 Americans. The year 1962, marked by the first use of helicopters on a massive scale, was a difficult one for the NLF; but it adjusted its tactics, while the strategic hamlets did not succeed in cutting it off from the population. In 1964–5, the NLF extended its control over the high plateaux and the central regions; by this time, the Diem regime had collapsed.
- 1965. The disintegration of South Vietnamese govern-

28. Indeed, the United States was active in Indochina as long ago as 1940–45.

29. By the beginning of 1968, the various allies of the United States had sent 55,000 men. According to official figures, the army loyal to the Saigon regime numbered 700,000.

ment forces led to a massive intervention by American troops. The dry season from October 1965 to May 1966 was marked by extremely bitter fighting, but the NLF managed to hold out and adjust to the new situation. Politically, the period was notable for the Buddhist crisis in Da Nang and Hue.

- In the second dry season, 1966–7, the NLF tightened its control over the main war zone (north of Hue, all the way up to the seventeenth parallel). All the fighting on the other side was done by the American forces, for there were widespread desertions among the South Vietnamese troops, whose fighting spirit was generally poor. This was the period of the major military operations code-named 'Junction City', 'Attleborough', etc.

- At the beginning of the third dry season (October 1967–May 1968) General Westmoreland, then commander-in-chief of the American forces, declared that his four-phase Plan had now reached Phase III. These four phases were defined as follows:

Phase I: Landing and deployment of American troops.
Phase II: Driving the 'Vietcong' back into the highlands.
Phase III: Destroying the 'Vietcong' infrastructure and entrusting the defence of a considerable part of the country – including the demilitarized zone – to the South Vietnamese army.
Phase IV: By 1969, starting to withdraw a considerable number of American troops from Vietnam.

The NLF offensive which began during the Tet truce and is still going on five months later has made this plan sound like empty propaganda – especially to the American people, who have been misled for so long about the results of 'pacification'.

In the liberated zones, over six million acres have been

distributed (at the rate of about seven acres per family). According to members of the NLF, the peasants are playing a more active role than in the war against the French, and the women's contribution is distinctly greater. At the present time, a *de facto* authority is being built up around the second NLF programme, which is a programme of national unity aimed at isolating the Americans and their partners. The Saigon government, which is profoundly corrupt (and seen as such, even by the American rulers), is in a vulnerable and precarious position.

The representativeness of the NLF seems likely to emerge as the key issue at the talks between the Americans and Vietnamese which opened in Paris in May 1968. South Vietnam's future is, after all, the kernel of the entire conflict.

Escalation

On 6 February 1965, a Soviet delegation headed by Mr Kosygin arrived in Hanoi. On 7 and 8 February, the US Air Force began the escalation of the war by bombing a large number of targets in the provinces of Vinh Linh and Quang Binh. 'Peaceful coexistence' was then at its height. On 10 February, Mr Kosygin signed a joint declaration condemning the American aggression and stated that he was ready to grant the Democratic Republic of Vietnam all the aid it needed in strengthening its defences.

In August 1964, the incident involving the USS *Maddox*, engaged on a spying mission in the Gulf of Tonkin, had given the Americans the excuse to intervene for the first time[30]. But this had been merely a warning shot.

After conflicting claims that it was (a) a rejoinder to the incident in the Gulf of Tonkin and (b) a reprisal for an attack on the American base at Pleiku, the Johnson administration asserted that escalation was designed to block the southward flow of troops and equipment from the DRV. Three years have now gone by, and it is patently not having the desired effect. The annual cost of escalation is put at $2,000 million: late in 1967, the American balance of payments deficit stood at more or less the same figure. In the seven years from 1961 to 1968, United States military estimates rose from $43,000 million to nearly $80,000 million.

A thirty-five-day pause in the bombing began on Christmas Eve 1965. Far from giving in, the Hanoi government hurriedly

30. This affair, the subject of mutual accusations at the time, now appears to have been far more clouded on the American side than was indicated by official circles at the time. cf. J. Amalric in *Le Monde*, 28 February 1968.

built up its anti-aircraft defences and made all possible preparations for withstanding a long siege[31].

Initially directed against the lines of communication, the raids soon spread to the industrial centres, the provincial capitals, the hospitals, the schools, and finally Haiphong and Hanoi.

Dispersal of resources and personnel was the most obvious way of countering the escalation. The surviving factories were broken down into smaller units and evacuated to country areas; the pattern of production was adjusted to suit the changing demands of the war effort; the provinces were encouraged to function independently. True, the economic life of the nation has been disturbed by the bombing, especially in the fields of industry and transport. But at the same time it has been stimulated by the psychological climate which always seems to thrive in a country whose independence is threatened. Destroyed communications have been restored on a deliberately reduced scale; bridges have been replaced and duplicated. Agricultural production has actually increased, even though a proportion of the rural labour force has been mobilized for other tasks. Thanks to the tactic of dispersal and to the construction of shelters for public and private use, the number of victims has been relatively small. Escalation has made North Vietnam a completely cohesive entity and increased its social dynamism.

31. cf. *Partisans*, No. 40, 'Le peuple vietnamien et la guerre', January-February 1968.

State and Village

The regime has not destroyed the village structure, with its cohesiveness and solidarity but has simply purged it of its more obvious built-in contradictions (the elders and land-owners). The commune was regarded as the logical point of departure for the co-operative. The Workers' Party was wise enough not to attempt to set up giant co-operatives combining dozens of villages, a policy which would have shattered their cohesiveness and taken away their sense of group security. The elders were got rid of, the landowners dispossessed, the common lands converted into co-operative estates. But the right to run the village co-operative independently has survived in large measure and been reinforced by the conditions imposed by the escalation of the war. The distinctive fellowship and unity of village life derive their strength today from communal labour on the collectively owned land. It must never be overlooked that the men who form the backbone of the party were once villagers themselves. In fact, the economic and cultural harmony of the village is perhaps even more marked than it was before; but the North Vietnamese rulers never aspired to use the traditional commune as the foundation for a 'Vietnamese socialism' based on the old mode of production. Socialism is an essentially modern phenomenon, differing from the traditional commune both in spirit and in patterns of organization; so old habits of work, and modern attitudes to it, need to be profoundly modified.

In the old days, the state used to collect its due without giving anything in return. 'You could travel all the way across the delta', writes Gourou, 'without encountering a single motorized vehicle or machine tool.' Today there is economic give-and-take. The peasants sell their surplus rice to the state, which is quick to make practical investments (e.g. pumping stations); they, in turn, buy consumer durables (e.g. thermos flasks, mosquito nets). Although Vietnam has been a national entity for hundreds of years, the predominant feeling until recently was one of solidarity at village level; patriotism was founded on links with the soil. There was no national market to foster national integration. Since independence, such a market has been brought to the smallest and remotest village, which is also kept in touch with the rest of the country by means of radio, the press, and party activities. So although escalation may have served to increase the autonomy of province and village, it has also given the peasants a previously unparalleled sense of being an integral part of a besieged nation. Patriotism and national pride have never been stronger in Vietnam than they are today.

The Role of Women

Part of the male labour force has been called up. This has quickened the rise in the status of women. There used to be a saying in Vietnam that 'a hundred girls aren't worth a single testicle'. The new regime has fought from the outset against polygamy and compulsory marriages, and it has given girls the same education as boys; but the pressures of war have probably won women greater advancement than all the years of peace-time put together. With the Party's encouragement, women have come to play a far more important role in production: the younger ones serve in the militia and have been fully trained for active service. The road-repair teams are largely made up of young girls spending a few days away from their parents' homes. The very attitude of the younger women, their whole way of thinking and looking at life, differs profoundly from the stand adopted by the previous generation. They are anxious to participate in everything; they assert themselves fearlessly; they want fewer children and more responsibilities. The conscious or unconscious reluctance to appoint women to higher posts has now vanished. New regulations came into force in 1967: an industrial unit or co-operative in which women make up 40 per cent of the labour force must have a woman on its management committee; when the figure reaches 50 per cent, the assistant manager must be a woman; 70 per cent or more, and the manager must be a woman.

Democratization at the Bottom

But perhaps the most significant change brought about by the prevailing wartime conditions is the increasing democratization of the regime. This process is now under way and has been actively encouraged by the Party leadership since April 1967. While centralization was still the aim, no real emphasis was laid on the need for the masses to participate in the running of factories and co-operatives[32]. But ordinary workers now play a greater part in working out local production plans.

Officials are required to give full consideration to any suggestions and criticisms made by the workers. The distribution of manufactured goods is carried out before the assembled members of the co-operative, in accordance with individual needs; the arrival of each new consignment is therefore publicly advertised, so that the products can be shared out in a democratic manner. The accounts are now examined at the

32. cf. Le Duan, *Sur la révolution socialiste au Vietnam* (Volume 3). 'Authority today takes the form of absolute rule by the proletariat. We are Communists, but many members of the Party still retain unfortunate vestiges of petty-bourgeois ideology. A number of them have made proletarian power a basis for despotic acts. That is why a stand must be made against individualism. It is imperative that the people's right of sovereignty be guaranteed. We have the constitution, originating with the Party leadership and extending from the cell to the highest level. The essential aim of the Party line and the Party's directives is to guarantee the people's right of sovereignty. But in practice there are times when this aim becomes distorted. Some of the blame lies with our cadres, but there is also another reason: the peasants and workers are not yet fully alive to their right to rule. Even in Hanoi, we haven't yet reached the point where every worker feels instinctively that his representatives are running the whole city, and that he shares in the responsibility for its management.' – *Former l'idéologie nouvelle pour construire le socialisme* (1962), pp. 85–90.

co-operative's general meeting, and revenue is regularly distributed instead of being withheld until after the harvest and then allocated according to a complicated points system; this means that accounts can be checked and, if need be, challenged. Until quite recently, the Party used to put up its own candidates for routine election to the People's Councils. Today, the workers are free to pick their own representatives. Indeed, the proportion of Party members elected to the People's Councils may no longer exceed 40 per cent – a limit which ensures that the masses participate in the administration of the commune. There have been attempts to put a stop to formal elections, in the belief that such a change would give fuller expression to the workers' aspirations.

In 1967 a three-month campaign was launched to rid the Party of dictatorial and excessively bureaucratic cadres, together with idlers and prevaricators. The hope was that a truly collective administration would follow. This campaign, conducted at every level, was resumed in 1968. Point IV in the directives issued on the occasion of the fiftieth anniversary of the October Revolution was: 'The campaign for democratization within the ranks of the people shall be carried on actively, so that production and the fighting effort may be intensified.'

Each member of the administrative committees or of the district parties is now responsible for the efficient running of a co-operative, while members of village committees are personally in charge of two or three production teams. Thus, officials are kept more directly informed about practical problems. They are required to appear in public once a month and listen to any criticisms which members of the co-operative may wish to level. Since this new system was adopted, the plots of land previously set aside for the administrative committees – about two and a half acres – have been done away with. Instead of the condemnations which used to be meted out for bad work, there is now praise for sound achievements. Everything is now discussed openly, so the workers feel personally involved – especially as the mobilization of the masses was accompanied by an improvement in the leadership of Party organizations. Moreover, all political cadres are now required to undergo technical or agricultural training courses, so that they may acquire a better knowledge of the problems instead of taking purely abstract and mechanical decisions about what ought to be done[33].

The changes I have mentioned certainly do not add up to self-management; still less do they herald the establishment of workers' councils. But this real phenomenon at village, district and, to a lesser extent, provincial level exists side by side with the centralization of authority.

These facts are not at all widely known. And yet they explain, over and above the historical and organizational reasons which I touched on earlier, why Vietnam is able to

33. Nguyen Khac Vien, *Démocratie nouvelle*, September 1967, 'Les 5 tonnes de Thai Binh': 'Previously, when things were going badly, we were content to haul the local officials over the coals. They would hang their heads and promise anything; we would go back to our offices, and the selfsame errors woulddoccur all over again. Finally we thought : "It is we at the top who are really to blame." So then we travelled out to the villages and co-operatives and said to the local officials: "Let us all put our heads together and see what is wrong, find out the causes and look for ways of putting things right: we are just as much to blame as you are." The local cadres and Party members began to think matters over, talk about them, examine themselves in a self-critical light, suggest solutions and pay more heed to the proposals put forward by the technical cadres. Then the same impulse spread to the masses. The young remembered that they had learned a good deal at school; and the old, uncommunicative until then, gave us the benefit of their experience. . . . A lot of resistance had to be broken down. We have barely emerged from a feudal society, and sometimes our cadres – in other words ourselves – are feudal-minded and hidebound in many matters, acting like elders or even betrayers of trust. On the one hand, then, it is essential to arouse enthusiasm and appeal to everyone's creative initiative; on the other, we must be capable of showing firmness and exercising discipline.' (Observations of the Party Secretary for Thai Binh province, pp. 17–18).

hold out. Since this campaign of democratization was launched, the co-operatives have been producing more. No national statistics have been published since 1965. But I established in the course of my special visit to the delta that both the total quantity of rice and the marketed surplus were higher than in 1965.

In previous years, some of the peasants had held their surplus back so as to sell it at a dearer rate for consumption at the Vietnamese New Year. In 1967, the co-operators took the matter into their own hands and placed restrictions on the people who were trying to speculate. It is noticeable that in the third quarter of 1967 prices on the free market were considerably lower than in the two previous years. Rice, for instance, valued at one dong in 1965, had gone up to two dongs in 1965 and three dongs in 1966. In the third quarter of 1967, the price fell to 1 dong 80. Naturally, some commodities are scarce. Among foodstuffs, there is a shortage of milk and fats. The monthly rice ration is thirty pounds for the general population, forty pounds for those engaged in particularly strenuous work, and forty-six pounds for the army. Townspeople are allowed five and a half yards of material a year, country people three and a quarter. But the dispersal of personnel has brought tens of thousands of cadres from Hanoi and Haiphong back into the provinces and villages, and this has led to a reduction in officialism and to greater national cohesiveness.

The Red River Delta

As Pierre Gourou writes:

Man is the most significant geographical factor in the delta. He has shaped its contours with his own hands. Apart from a few lone hills, the outstanding features of the plain are the dikes. The vegetation spread over these six thousand square miles is never natural. Not an inch of forest land, at times not even a copse. Because of their religious value, a few tiny sacred groves are permitted to retain a tight cluster of trees and a semblance of undergrowth; but it would not take long to draw up a complete list of these meagre islets of natural vegetation. Tall trees are a rarity, and even the mangoes and small shade-trees become less and less frequent as one approaches the sea. With these few exceptions, all the vegetation is domestic. The bamboo hedges are the object of man's care and development. Every particle of soil has been tilled again and again, and even the grass growing on the narrow dikelets is conscientiously trimmed and used for fodder. Only the cemeteries are left untouched: unassuming mounds show where the graves are, and man's presence is even stronger here than in the fields where the crops are growing.

The landscape has altered since these lines were written, thirty years ago. The paddy-fields, which were divided into tiny plots before collectivization, now lie in long straight lines, with rationally determined boundaries. There are many more dikes and dikelets than in the past, and the canal system is far more extensive. Pumping stations have taken the place of the old, irksome scoops. Young trees line the roads: Japanese lilacs, their slim trunks topped with clustering leaves; banyans and longans, hiding army lorries and Sam missiles. Eucalypti grow on soil which was once eroded, and between the scrupulously manured paddy-fields filaos spring up beside the high-tension wires linking the pumping stations. On the banks of the lakes and ponds stand willows (a feminine symbol in Vietnamese poetry) and coconut palms – southern trees serving as reminders of the divided nation.

Part of the province of Ha Tay is made up of hulking lime-stone mountain masses whose peaks are remarkably level with one another; the steep hills have been retimbered. The provinces of Hung Yen and Thai Binh, on the other hand, are completely flat. The only salient features are the results of human handiwork: dikes, aircraft-observation posts, stupas dating back to the time of the Khmers. There are paddy-fields everywhere, looking intensely green on the eve of the 'tenth-month harvest'; also jute, with its slender, graceful stalks. But water is the key element in the delta: grey in the dawn mist as a sampan glides along between the reeds; muddy in the workaday task of irrigation; catching the light in lakes and pools, among the lotuses, the hyacinths, the duckweed.

In addition, the war has created its own landscape: buildings flattened or blasted open in even the smallest provincial centres; gaping bridges; pitted roads. Nothing has been spared, neither hospitals and schools nor pagodas and churches.

A good many observers have already described this aspect of the war, both in Phat Diem and Thanh Hoa, which I was able to visit, and in the area farther south, along the seventeenth parallel. During those weeks towards the end of 1967, the war was omnipresent in North Vietnam – even in Hanoi, which had been spared in previous years. I was in the capital on 26, 27 and 28 October, when the bombing raids reached a peak of violence. About 150 dwellings[34] were destroyed, and according to Vietnamese sources there were 200 dead and injured; thirty American planes were brought down, and five pilots taken prisoner.

34. Principally in the rue Tran Quoc Toan and in the following streets or neighbourhoods: Hoang Dien, Cua Bec, Thuy Khe, Nguyen Trung To.

The outward appearance of the Vietnamese village has undergone two sets of changes since the war of national liberation. The years of peace brought septic tanks, hygienically protected wells and, in some places, houses built of solid materials with threshing floors outside each home. And now the years of war have brought individual dugouts along the roads leading to the fields, air-raid shelters, protective walls, and trenches dug directly under people's beds.

Most of the houses have thatched roofs and mud walls; the upright supports are made from the wood of areca palms. The interiors consist of one large rectangular room containing an altar for the worship of ancestors, two or three beds with mosquito netting (these have taken the place of the old straw mattresses), and a table on which sons and daughters do their homework and parents do their accounts.

In country districts, the children set out for school armed with their blue plastic satchels, their first-aid kits and their plaited straw helmets. Along the roads, whatever the weather, young men and girls are busy repairing the battered surfaces. And when evening comes, the lines of lorries pour southwards like a black river, bearing their loads of men and materials.

In North Vietnam, the battle to maintain communications has been won by the population as a whole, and agricultural production has continued to rise in spite of the bombing. In South Vietnam, the foreign presence – added to the incompetence and corruption of the Saigon administration – has gradually earned the NLF the support of social groups and religious sects which used to be hostile to it. This development, which began soon after the collapse of the Buddhist movement as a third force in 1965–6, is the reason for the Front's new programme of national unity, which is designed to increase the Americans' isolation in the south.

By her determination, Vietnam has slowly but surely warded off the disadvantages which she might have suffered as a result of the dispute between China and Russia. The Soviet Union has been induced to step up its aid, despite its reluctance to become involved – even indirectly – in the Vietnam war.

The start of preliminary talks between the United States and North Vietnam in the spring of 1968 and the decision to stop bombing north of the nineteenth parallel show that the Johnson administration has come to realize, in the aftermath of the Tet offensive, that the escalation of the war is simply not producing the desired results. Nevertheless, the US Air Force is now hammering the area between the seventeenth and nineteenth parallels harder than ever.

Obviously, the principal point at issue in the Paris talks is the representativeness of the NLF[35], which is the only organization putting up an armed fight, and therefore the only organization giving practical expression to the longing for national independence felt by the people of South Vietnam.

The purpose of the raids on North Vietnam was not purely military: the whole idea of a war which would somehow spare the civilian population and destroy only strategic targets is a fiction which does not stand up to examination[36]. The bombing was also intended to demoralize ordinary citizens until, directly or indirectly, they pressurized the Hanoi government into suing for peace. The US Air Force has deliberately directed some of its attacks against the civilian population. But there is another way of killing people, and that is by undoing the hard, patient work of many years. In a world whose basic problem is surely the backwardness and penury of two thirds of the planet, the United States government – whatever excuses it may invoke – has systematically destroyed the economic infra-

35. The guerrilla strategy employed by the N.L.F. deserves separate study – especially the Front's activities in the towns and cities. The urban and rural campaigns have been carefully synchronized – a clear break with the pattern established in China.

36. cf. the findings of the Russell Tribunal recorded in *Le Jugement de Stockholm*, Gallimard, Paris, 1967.

structure of one of the three or four 'underdeveloped' countries which have seriously laid the foundations for their own industrialization. There can be no comparison between a bridge or factory built with the resources of an industrial nation and a similar project undertaken by a country which is still agricultural and which finds it hard to make ends meet. Anyone aware of the patience, initiative and hardship entailed in any attempt at self-improvement will realize that what the US Air Force has been destroying is not characterless 'strategic targets', but the blood and sweat of the North Vietnamese people. In the view of most countries – especially the newer ones – the American intervention in Vietnam is an attempt to stifle national independence and dignity.

1. The Province of Hung Yen

Tuan Doanh, member of the Provincial Committee of the Workers' Party:

How ever do we manage to keep going? Here we are, with the war at its height – yet not only are we fighting, we're building socialism as well. Few people, even in the socialist camp, can make out how we have achieved such a victory. 'You can be told about a thing a hundred times,' says our President, Ho Chi Minh. 'It is better to see it just once.' I don't know whether life was all that much harsher in Hung Yen than anywhere else in the old days, but I'll tell you a story that used to go the rounds in these parts: it seems a girl from another province married one of our villagers; she loved him, but after a few weeks she left him because the work was far too hard. In those days, people's working lives were so arduous that husband and wife ate only one meal a day and spent only half the night together; could anybody call that marriage? You had to be up at cockcrow – three in the morning, say – and you didn't get home till nine at night. The province was so poor that it used to be known as Beggars' Province. The Red River dam would burst at times, and when that happened the entire province was flooded. It might be six months before the waters went down.

Rushes and reeds grew everywhere; the whole area was a swamp. The peasants of Hung Yen had to leave the province and move to Laos and Thailand. Some even emigrated to Guiana and New Caledonia. Those who stayed behind were so poor that they could not even build temples in honour of the spirits that were supposed to watch over their villages. They were weighed down with debts, many of which were handed on from generation to generation.

After 1945, dikes were erected. This kept the water in check and ruled out the risk of flooding; but we were afflicted with droughts instead, for there were no supply mains. This situation lasted until 1958. When the north-west wind blew, the children were able to play marbles on the dried-up river-bed. We had a saying in those days: 'For five months of the year, we use our feet for getting about; for seven months we use our arms [i.e. we row].' In times of drought the peasants had to rely on scoops, bailing water and moistening the soil as and when they could. They dug wells to a depth of twenty or twenty-five feet so that they could irrigate with the aid of buckets. It was very hard work and they were hungry all the time. Our province was so poor that the number of illiterates rose to 98 per cent.

In the old days, before the French came, Chinese was widely taught; but afterwards education came to a standstill, for there was only one elementary school per district.

Historically, our province has been a battlefield ever since the days of the Trung and Trieu sisters, in the second and third centuries. The marshes and reeds provided an excellent terrain for guerrilla warfare in the lowlands, and the dense vegetation stopped the enemy from advancing. There were also major battles against the Mongols in the thirteenth century. It is fair to say that the peasants of Hung Yen have had to withstand continual attempts at invasion throughout their history, in addition to long periods of drought and flooding. They've had the French to contend with, too! It was the Scholars who organized a resistance movement in the villages. There is not a single village in these parts which did not play a part in the resistance. That was in my grandfather's day, and he did his share. It was a peasant uprising on a really large scale, and even the women fought.

The French tracked down the graves containing the ancestors of hostile mandarins, and proceeded to scatter the bones: they aimed to undermine our morale by preventing us from practising ancestor-worship. But nobody talked: they didn't find out any of the things they wanted to know. After the defeat of the Scholars, one of the ringleaders who had somehow managed to survive organized a rebellion in the province of Bac Giang. All in all, the resistance against the French was kept up for over twenty years; but the rising was doomed to failure, of course, for we lacked both the ideological weapons and the material means of resistance.

The first Party cell in the province was set up in 1930. Of the five founder members, one is still alive: he is now a man of seventy. There was a really severe wave of repression from 1931 until 1933, and they were unable to make any headway in those years. Between 1933 and 1940 they established contact with the general population and began to build up a mass following, and in 1940 the Party was properly restructured at provincial level. From 1936 until 1939 the Party was allowed to function openly and lawfully, within certain limits. It was able to hold a number of public meetings at which future policies were discussed. There was a good deal more talk about landownership than about independence: it was 'democratic freedoms' that the Party was pressing for in those days. The colonial government readopted its repressive measures in 1939; but the Party was fully prepared for this eventuality, having retained its clandestine set-up even while outwardly operating within the framework of the law. By 1940, repression or no repression, we were able to get on with our propaganda work and agitation. Each militant was required to establish contact with several villages, propagate a certain number of ideas and watchwords, and do his best to establish nests of sympathizers. This went on from 1940 until 1944. There were very few professional revolutionaries in the area – no more than four or five in the entire province; the rest did ordinary jobs as well as working for the Party. And then, round about 1943 or 44, we started making military preparations. On a very small scale, mind: we had no arms and ammunition as yet. We simply made a theoretical study of how to handle weapons. All our military leaders were trained in this way. We were getting ready for the fray.

On 9 March 1945 came the Japanese *coup* toppling the colonial administration. Our people promptly attacked the French military post at Ban, on Road 5, which was held by a platoon of forty; we seized a quantity of arms and ammunition. The second attack was directed against a regional centre. The French were in such disarray that they could do nothing to stop us. Side by side with the armed conflict, the masses were incited to lay hands on the stocks of rice held by the Japanese. It must be remembered that there was an acute shortage of food at the time. Other stocks had been built up by the elders and landowners. The latter, including French landowners, amounted to only 3 per cent of the population, yet owned 70 per cent of the land. One of them owned about 750 acres. He was a Frenchman. The leading Vietnamese landowners held over 500 acres. The communal rice-stocks in the possession of the village elders were, in theory, intended for the poor. They were shared out, together with the supplies appropriated by the Japanese. In addition, all taxes were withheld. As a result of these steps, starvation was averted in the province. In other parts of the country, where these popular risings did not reach the same proportions, famine conditions prevailed. This seizure of rice for public use finally removed the peasants' uncertainties about the revolution. The atmosphere was such that people would storm any rice convoy on sight, often without the slightest planning or organization. We commandeered all the rice we could, and all the weapons.

In August 1945, we took over every district in the land. The people in this area advanced on the main town in a twelve-mile procession and claimed it as their own. Every single town and village was in the hands of militants – it was a nationwide take-over of power. You couldn't move, there were so many people. Suddenly we found ourselves enjoying independence and freedom. The mood of the country was unbelievable: people were burning with enthusiasm. I shall never forget those times.

And then, in December, the French invaded us again. They occupied the northern half of the province so as to secure control of Road 5, which runs from Hanoi to Haiphong. In December 1949 they realized that the war was going to be a long one, so they occupied the southern half of the province as well. 'Pacification' started once they had taken over the whole province. They set up 480 posts in 675 villages – in other words, four posts to every three square miles. To maintain their hold on Road 39, they destroyed 130 villages which lay along it or near it. By the end of the war they had bombarded and destroyed 534 villages. And they employed every conceivable form of terrorism, all over the province. In Van Nhuc, for example, they rounded up the best part of 300 people and shot them all; that was in 1950. In one Catholic village, they killed 350 people on New Year's Day; and they killed 450 in the church at Tan Nhan, during a Sunday bombardment. In the village of Dong Tao they seized forty-two young people, tortured them and hanged them from the banyan trees.

After 1949 the people living in the delta became the focal point of their attentions. They needed to raise volunteers for the puppet army. But by then they had engaged in too many forms of extortion. The military posts had come to be known as 'slaughterhouses'. Hundreds of people were killed in these posts, and a great many more were tortured. Yet despite this reign of terror, our army and cadres could not be dislodged; the peasants continued to hide them. A complete network of underground shelters and communication trenches was established, stretching for tens of miles, with exits in or on the outskirts of villages. As the war dragged on, it became possible to conceal and accommodate whole regiments and, eventually, whole divisions.

The French set up puppet municipal councils, staffed with collaborators. It was our task to smash these councils. So we turned the villages into military strongholds, barricading them and digging underground passages. Sometimes a guerrilla platoon was able to withstand a siege by an enemy regiment. After dark, parties of our men would go and harass enemy posts defended by entire battalions. It was early in 1951 that we embarked on a new offensive strategy, besieging the weaker posts and bypassing the stronger ones: this was known as 'leapfrogging'. Guerrilla warfare spread northwards through the province to a point not far from Hanoi airport. Our regional forces rose to a strength equivalent to two regiments. Each district had a company, and we had our own guerrilla unit operating at village level.

In 1951 the French, under General de Lattre, began to employ 'mobile groups' [*groupes mobiles*, often referred to as GMs]. Our own army was made up of 'mobile groups', too. They sent three GMs into the eastern part of the province, knowing that the area contained a strong build-up of forces.

Their plan was to scour the zone and drive the guerrillas back into the highlands, so that the population of the delta could be brought to heel. The mobile groups were extremely well-trained, and they were dangerous. They gave us a lot of trouble at first, but with the support of the general population we gradually managed to get the better of them, despite our shortage of arms and ammunition. In the meantime, we had slowly but surely knocked out the smaller military posts; only the really big ones were left, and after a while the troops defending them began to lose morale. On one occasion – round about 1953, if my memory serves me right – one of these larger posts was captured under cover of darkness. It was manned by puppet forces, and the trunks of banana trees had been dressed up to look like artillery. We didn't need to fire a shot. They thought we must have heavy armaments with us, so they surrendered.

In the early days, before the enemy lost control, we had to plant some of our own people inside the elders' councils and also liquidate some of the existing elders. We were politically active among the general population, and it was they who urged the elders to oppose the rates and taxes. Our efforts in this direction enabled us to hide in the villages while the French were combing a given area, for some of the elders had been won over to our cause.

By the time the battle of Dien Bien Phu began, there were only thirty posts left in the province of Hung Yen. They were like small islands in a Vietminh ocean. When supplies had to be sent to a post, the French would employ whole battalions to open up the roads. And they weren't content to attack us militarily: they attacked us economically as well. They killed the people working in the fields. They killed the cattle – machine-gunning our buffaloes, for instance. They destroyed our tools. It was no longer possible to work by day, so the peasants worked during the hours of darkness. As lamps, they used glow-worms imprisoned in bladders; burning joss-sticks showed where the fields ended. And once the mass killing of buffaloes started, the ploughs were drawn by human beings.

We also had more than our share of difficulties about arms

and ammunition. At first we used to send people to collect them from the highlands; but there was a risk these men and women might get caught, and in the end we found it easier to steal from the French. The French Expeditionary Force became principal supplier to our local and provincial forces. We had a repair shop, and other workshops chiefly devoted to the manufacture of mines. When peace came, the French bequeathed us dozens of tons of barbed wire and tens of thousands of mines.

Afterwards, we had to patch up the wounds of war. Land reform became the key issue. It was imperative that a large-scale peasant movement should be directed against the landowners; but this was hard to achieve, for the latter had set up organizations which exercised a powerful influence over some of the population. I should perhaps add that on the revolutionary side the cadres were all operating under cover, and that the political education of masses and militants alike was of an extremely low standard. Matters reached such a pitch that there was not always a clear dividing line between the revolutionary organizations and the reactionary organizations run by the landowners; and as our cadres kept their identities concealed and often had little first-hand knowledge of the villages, the masses had difficulty in telling friend from foe at times – especially in view of the dictatorial conduct of some of the cadres. So there was considerable mental confusion, resulting in many mistakes . . .

We had a really bitter struggle with the landowners over the abolition of feudal tenure. Here again, mistakes were made. Landowners were unjustly accused, and attacks were directed against Party members and other proven patriots. Later, the Party publicly acknowledged that errors had been committed on a nation-wide scale. Every branch of the Party studied the records closely to see where these errors lay. Yet, in spite of all these mistakes, the land reform programme worked. Never before had the peasants been able to call the land their own. Production swiftly exceeded the prewar level. In the years 1958–60 the first mutual-aid co-operatives were set up. Extensive developments in irrigation were put in hand. Canal-cutting began. On 15 January 1958, President Ho visited our province.

He pointed out that the province had suffered nine droughts in ten years, and insisted on the urgent need for improved water management. He suggested we cut a four-mile canal. We mustered the population of three districts to carry out the digging, and the President walked along the proposed line of the canal, to indicate the path it was to follow. We dug up 80,000 cubic yards of earth. It took two months – 220,000 working days. In the early stages, people's hearts were not really in the project, and so the output was poor – less than half a cubic yard per person per day. But after the canal was opened, the paddy-fields on either side yielded two harvests a year instead of one, and we nicknamed it 'Uncle Ho's Canal'. There is a little song which runs:

> In Uncle Ho's Canal,
> The water is bright and clear.
> The rice and maize grow strong.
> The hungry days are gone.

Afterwards we cut a five-mile canal in twenty days – 290,000 cubic yards, with a labour force drawn from a single district. Having solved the drought problem, the southern [i.e. lowland] villages proceeded to tackle the problem of flooding. More and more dikes and dikelets were built once the peasants saw how effective they were, and there was a general increase in yield. Campaigns were also launched to raise the educational standards of the cadres and of the general population, and to raise a strong militia for national defence.

Privately owned property did not exceed an acre and a quarter per household, and this area was made of several small plots. There was no way of getting water to a particular plot without conveying it across others, and the peasants were well aware that this was not a sensible arrangement. In 1958 we began to launch co-operatives. About 12 per cent of peasant households had joined by the end of that year, and 23 per cent by the end of 1959. The May–June harvest of 1959 produced a low yield, because of bad weather, and about 10 per cent of those who had joined the co-operatives asked to leave. At this juncture, the Party promoted a nation-wide discussion about whether it was better to work individually or as a team. Every village took part in this debate, which went on for two months. It aroused intense interest. People who had never participated in discussions instigated by the Party now spoke up, not only at meetings but in private arguments. In the end, co-operation won the day. After this campaign, the 10 per cent who had previously wanted to leave withdrew their applications. New members poured in. Nearly half our people had joined co-operatives by 1960, or thereabouts. There was a good harvest at the end of the year, and this certainly helped. By the beginning of 1961, 91 per cent of the peasants in this province were members of co-operatives.

There was one old man who never attended meetings. Eventually a discussion was held near his home, and he heard the speakers referring to his own plot of land: they were saying it was cultivated in such-and-such a manner. At this, he wandered over and listened. It so happened that in the course of the day he had visited a number of plots which were under co-operative management. He felt that the comments being made about the quality of these plots were quite wrong, and he said so. We invited him to join in the debate. He spent several evenings talking things over with us – he even brought his wife along. In the end, we won him over.

Let me tell you of another peasant who was reluctant to join. Like the first, he shunned our debates; indeed, he wouldn't have anything to do with our militants and the members of the co-operative. One day he felled a tree and was unable to shift it without help. We turned a blind eye at first, but at the end of the day one of the comrades lent him a hand. 'You see,' this comrade said, 'there *is* something to be said for collective labour . . .' And with that he walked away. Well, next morning the old man came to see us and said: 'I've been thinking. I've talked it over with my wife, and I reckon you're right. I'm going to give the co-operative a try.'

In 1965, our irrigation and drainage system was further improved. Six and a half million cubic yards were excavated – about 150 per cent more than in 1964. Nine million cubic yards were excavated in the first six months of 1966 alone. And the canals operating in this province now extend to over 23,000 miles, which is almost the length of the equator. Many new pumping stations have been built: at the beginning of 1965 – before escalation began – we had thirty-three; today, after two and a half years of resistance, we have 120. Side by side with these developments in irrigation, we have built a high-tension electric system (thirty-five kilovolts) and a local network (ten kilowatts). We have 250 miles of lines, with four hundred small power plants (electricity and diesel) – and this in spite of the air-strikes!

Here in Hung Yen, we produce 687 pounds of rice per head per year. We have also started growing jute – a new venture, this. Fifteen thousand acres are given over to it, producing 11,000 tons or two thirds of the nation's jute. As for longans, prior to 1960 we exported seventy tons: today we export 700. In 1963 we exported twenty tons of oranges: in 1966 we exported 500 tons. In this sphere, we are the second most successful province in the country.

We keep a bare minimum of bullocks and buffaloes, for we have no pasture lands. There are 230 thousand pigs, distributed among 120 thousand peasant households, an average of two pigs per household. The total area devoted to fish-breeding is hard to assess: everybody has a pond.

Industrial output and the work of skilled craftsmen accounted for 20 per cent of total production in 1964. They accounted for 47 per cent in 1966. The number of workshops has multiplied tenfold since the raids made it necessary for us to disperse our industrial activities. Some of the engineering works are quite small. We have set up 400 miniature repair shops and workshops of various kinds. The jute which used to be exported is now converted into sacking right here in Hung Yen, and all the fruit we produce is canned locally too. We have our own paper factory. The autonomy of the province is increasing all the time. In 1964 we had fewer than a thousand industrial workers; in 1967 we have 8,000. What we chiefly lack at present is a sufficient number of technically qualified people at managerial level. The labour force is made up of peasants who have been swiftly retrained. Most of them have received general education – six or seven classes – and this makes it easier for them to cope with the technical courses. Until the late 1950s the peasants were less well housed and fed than the workers and cadres, which gave rise to jealousy. But now they can afford to feel sorry for the cadres, for the position has been reversed. Rationing is less of a problem for the peasant, he being a producer. In 1965 the peasants in this province bought eighteen million dongs-worth of goods from the state; in 1966 they bought twenty-four million dongs-worth, with no increase in prices – clothing materials, thermos flasks, oils of various kinds ... Savings-bank deposits were 150 per cent higher in 1966 than in 1965.

A total of 210,000 children are receiving general education, which begins in the nursery schools and finishes at Class 10. Each commune has a first-phase school (four classes), a second-phase school (three classes) and a third-phase school (likewise three classes). We have 30,000 pupils staying on until they reach Class 7, and 8,000 in the third-phase schools. Two thousand completed their studies this year. We have 6,700 teachers. In addition to all this, 60,000 adults are attending evening classes. One out of every two members of the population is engaged in some form of study. The communal cadres are working their way through the second-phase course, or currently completing it. There are also vocational schools, farming schools, engineering schools, teachers' training colleges, and schools turning out qualified medical auxiliaries. Specialized instruction is available in hydraulic engineering and fish-breeding. We have 300 provincial cadres taking university courses. We have ten graduates in economic planning, thirty agronomists, forty doctors who are also qualified surgeons, five industrial engineers. And we have two professional artistic groups in the province.

Since escalation began, our dikes have been attacked a few times; but the craters have been filled in without much difficulty. Seven aircraft have been brought down over the province. Sixty thousand young people have left, some to join the army, others to work in industry or on the roads; 10,000 of them are girls. Seventy thousand inhabitants have moved to the highlands, to relieve congestion in the delta; this is part of a carefully planned policy.

In spite of the war, the transformations brought about in the past ten years are continuing. We are transforming nature, transforming human beings, transforming the pattern of living. If the people who left in 1954 were to return today, they would not recognize the province. There has been a radical change in outlook, and this has been brought about mainly by ideological, political means. A collective morality is beginning to take root. Each individual is working for himself and for everyone else as well. The old regime was characterized by a complete lack of democracy and the absence of all things modern. Today we have democracy, and we also have machinery, electricity and improvements in irrigation.

In theory, 'only sons' are exempt from military service; but many families see this as a slur on their honour and insist that their sons have a right to serve their country. Some boys attempt to lie their way into the army at sixteen. Those who are under-weight or not tall enough demand certificates to show that they have been turned down; a number of them bluff their way past the authorities. Joining up is a much sought-after honour.

The Americans' hopes were misplaced: far from being worse off, we are better off economically and in terms of morale. The same impulses which helped us to beat the French colonialists are now helping us to beat the American imperialists.

Setting up co-operatives was an essential preliminary to increasing production. The peasants were not opposed to them, but getting them to join was not exactly easy. We also had to teach them how to organize labour and improve their yield, and this was extremely complicated. At first the peasant adopted the same attitude as in the days when he had worked for a landowner: in other words he took his time. This led to a drop in yield, which in turn prompted doubts and uncertainties not only among the peasants but among the cadres who initially backed the co-operative system. Some of the cadres working in the province said: 'After the land reform programme has been carried out, we must allow private ownership to develop and they must learn to improve production.' They were rather sceptical about the success of the co-operatives. Had the Party leadership wavered at that moment (1959), the entire process would have gone into reverse.

The co-operatives were like those young shoots which attract blight in their early days. Not all of them ran into trouble; a few worked quite well. What we tried to do was seek out the most successful and discover *why* they were successful. We found four on high ground and four on low, employing different methods of cultivation. We immediately packed our cadres off to see what these co-operatives had to teach us. Then we called the heads of the other co-operatives together and explained why things were going well in the more dynamic areas. Next we compared working methods. We made every attempt to find out whether the root of the trouble lay in the rules and regulations or in the style of management – which might, for instance, be too dictatorial. Later we made arrangements for the managerial staff from other co-operatives to visit these successful districts. At every stage, we all did our best to discover exactly how things were done; we made comparison after comparison, in the hope of learning why some co-operatives worked better than others.

Subsequently the general trend was for co-operatives to switch from monoculture to mixed farming, with the right to sell surplus produce on the commercial market. This was no longer a political problem, but a scientific and technical problem. Those of us who held positions of responsibility were not agronomists. We were short of technicians, and the few we could call on had little experience. We didn't underestimate the technicians, but I must point out that they had been trained abroad and lacked sufficient first-hand knowledge of Vietnamese conditions to provide the solutions we needed. So we decided that it was up to the leadership to join the technicians in seeking the answers to specific local difficulties. By 1962 the irrigation problems were solved and other technical problems came to the fore: the vagaries of the climate, for instance. The end-of-the-year rice crop grows throughout the summer. Summer was said to be the best season, while the traditional belief was that spring was the best time for growing. In practice, the main effort is still directed towards the end-of-the-year crop. Until then, it was the 'tenth-month harvest' which yielded the best crop in our province. But now that we had solved the water problem, we could count on two harvests. Hitherto the peasants had gone on supposing that the summer rice which grows in the dry season was a risky proposition. But the recent irrigation improvement presented the matter in an entirely new light. The rice was not treated with sufficient care, for people did not seriously expect a good crop. So at this juncture the views of leadership and peasants were diametrically opposed. To stake everything on the end-of-the-year harvest was to perpetuate monoculture and gamble on the weather – for although it might be the rainy season, the rains did not always come when they were most needed. There was a danger of drought as well as flooding, and typhoons had often to be reckoned with too. On the other hand, the winter–spring [i.e. dry-season] rice-crop presented only one problem: lack of water. So once the irrigation programme was completed, the whole position changed. The peasants could not see this. In 1963 we decided, after taking careful stock, that the dry season should become the principal season because it had the greatest number of factors in its favour. Naturally it was hard for the peasants to accept this idea, but we made an all-out effort to put it across. Although the new system ran directly counter to the traditional view, it produced results; the facts proved us right. We explained the advantages of the decision, re-educating and reorganizing the population, and it is on this basis that agriculture is now developing. Agricultural experts helped us in our campaign: our leaders had only to raise a problem, and the technicians would make a scientific analysis and find the appropriate answers. The men at the top became more knowledgeable in scientific and technical matters. At the same time, every attempt was made to draw on the experience of the older peasants. The agricultural experts were asked to talk things over with them – though, of course, we did not hesitate to fly in the face of traditional ideas when we considered them unscientific.

Thus, we in Hung Yen eventually arrived at a system of mixed farming. We now grow a variety of crops: jute, maize, soya and haricot beans, sugar-cane, sweet potato . . . We have also made progress in husbandry, especially pig and poultry keeping. Until 1954, Hung Yen was a purely agricultural region, with no timber, no minerals, not a scrap of industry. We were just a granary. The thought of this became an obsession with our leaders. Matters were further complicated by the fact that none of us had a clear idea of what industry really was. We looked into the question of local craftsmanship and found that the province had produced its share of craftsmen in earlier centuries; so we were perfectly capable of doing something other than farming. Industry soon becomes indispensable to rapia agricultural development; without it, in our view, all attempts to secure a better yield from the land must inevitably fail. So we looked around to see how industry had developed in other countries and in our own industrial provinces. We toured other areas, and it seemed to us that the problem was not insoluble. There were similar conditions elsewhere, and they had not proved a bar to industry. As a first step, we started manufacturing our own farming tools. As a second step, we improved our methods of conveyance; we felt these were holding us up, so we began to produce carts fitted with lorry-tyres, also wheelbarrows (there were none here in the old days). And as a third step, we have tried to evolve towards mechanization. The manufacture of complete machinery is beyond us as yet, but we can – and do – manufacture components: spare parts for diesel pumps, for instance, and for the other equipment at the pumping stations. If we were to wait for the central factories, it would be months before we received all the components we need here. We then set to work and tried to manufacture threshing-machines and huskers. Next we established our own food-processing plants, for here again the central factories could not keep pace with demand.

There have been major developments in the educational field, too – for socialism demands high technical and cultural standards. We worked hard to do away with illiteracy, but this was not enough. Somehow the cultural level had to be raised and production increased. In 1961 the general population began to build schools. We trained our own teachers, and today the cultural and technical standards of the population are distinctly higher than they were five years ago.

Then again, an efficient medical service is essential if production and national defence are to be maintained. Naturally the demands on this service have increased since the air raids began. The provincial authorities are responsible for running it and keeping it up to standard. Today we have a unit in every village, with a medical auxiliary and a midwife. At district level, we have a hospital staffed by a doctor and several medical auxiliaries. And at provincial level we have a central hospital, with a team of highly skilled surgeons who are capable of dealing with even the most intricate cases. Very little surgery is performed in Hanoi these days, apart from a few brain and heart operations.

As for ideological leadership, after the mistakes of the land reform programme the population thought: 'We must no longer look for wealth, we must be content to rub along.' Those who had savings made every attempt to hide them, paying nothing into their bank accounts. Production fell off badly. In 1962 we launched a campaign urging the province of Hung Yen to grow rich and celebrate. Our message was that, working within the collectivist orbit, people should aim to reap wealth for themselves, their families, their co-operatives and their country. The older peasants said: 'The Party sees right into our hearts.' Previously they had devoted little time or attention to their private allotments, for they were uncertain of the future; but now they began to work hard, both for the co-operatives and for themselves. Cuttings began to appear everywhere, and there was a genuine air of celebration. Obviously, conditions have been difficult since escalation started. We have called for an extra effort, and by stepping up production the peasants are playing their part in the war against aggression. This has prompted a spirit of rivalry: they all go along to the public meetings and say what they have done. We feel this answers a psychological need in the peasants. If they have achieved something, they want people to know about it. And their efforts are also remunerated in accordance with a points system. This combination of material and psychological rewards seems to us a wise formula.

The Province of Hung Yen

A few facts:

The province of Hung Yen lies in the middle of the Red River delta: it owes its origins to the river's alluvial deposits.

It covers an area of 360 square miles and has 650,000 inhabitants. Administratively it is divided into nine districts and a chief town. There are 155 communes, of which ninety-six border upon the Red River or its tributary, the Luoc. The total number of villages is 679.

Hung Yen has an upper region – twenty-three feet above sea-level – in the north. In the south (give or take a few elevations not exceeding twenty feet) is the low-lying region, a mere six feet above sea-level. Until recently, the higher ground could be cultivated only in the rainy season and the lower ground only in the dry season. The intermediate zone did not always retain sufficient rain in the dry season for it to be drained in the rainy season so that it might produce two harvests a year. The slightest drought, the least excess of rain, and the harvest was lost. Hydraulic developments, especially in the sphere of drainage, made it possible to overcome these difficulties. Single-harvest rice has been replaced, on the higher ground, by dry industrial crops[1].

On the eve of the land reform programme (1954), the peasantry of Hung Yen could be subdivided, according to Vietnamese classifications, as in Table 7.

After the mistakes of the land reform programme had been set right, three trial co-operatives were set up in 1958. During the winter of 1958–9, 222 co-operatives came into being,

1. See Nguyen Khac Vien's article, 'L'eau, le riz, les hommes', published in *Etudes vietnamiennes*, No. 2, 1964, pp. 8–44. See also the report on the province of Hung Yen by the colonial administrator Miribel (1901).

regrouping 3.2 per cent of the population. In 1959, lectures on the future of the farming co-operative were given by Party officials to 25,000 militants, communal cadres and representatives of people's organizations.

Table 7.

Category	Number of households	Number of persons
Landowners	3,535	17,013
Rich peasants	1,913	11,904
Average peasants	44,846	208,775
Poor and landless peasants	88,829	346,911

In 1959 there were 1,207 co-operatives, accounting for 54 per cent of the population. In spite of a poor harvest, the co-operatives increased in number – thanks to a huge campaign explaining the advantages they offered. In 1960, 93 per cent of the population were working for 1,408 co-operatives. The improved irrigation and drainage soon had the desired effect, and it became possible to bring in two harvests a year instead of one. In 1961 the co-operative movement came to full fruition.

Table 8. Development of production in Hung Yen.

	1957	1962	1966
Rice production (in tons)	153,240	18,070	191,962
Area devoted to jute (in acres)	2,083	9,256	13,889
Food production (in millions of dongs)	37.6	46	47.1
Value of industrial crops (in millions of dongs)	2.3	4.61	5.4
Stock-farming (in millions of dongs)	7.6	14	—

Table 9. Breakdown of agricultural income (in millions of dongs).

	Food crops	Industrial crops	Stock-farming	Fish-breeding	Others
1957	37.6	3.3	7.6	0	12.6
1962	46	4.61	14	1.8	15.9
1966	47.1	5.4	—	—	—

The Village of Quoc Tri

A few facts:

Quoc Tri is a village in the low-lying region of Hung Yen. It used to flood during the rainy season. The formation of the co-operative made a large collective labour force available, and the substantial system of dikes which this labour force built now enables the village to bring in two harvests a year.

The village contains a considerable number of stone-built houses, complete with tiled threshing-floors. There is an electricity supply (thirty-five kilowatts), but this is used solely for the technical needs of the co-operative and for the loud-speakers along the village streets.

The population is put at 4,200, including 2,700 women; the exact number of men is not available. Fifteen hundred children are receiving education. The first- and second-phase classes have a teaching staff of thirty-eight. The medical team consists of two medical auxiliaries and eleven nurses and midwives.

In 1960, the number of Party members totalled 218. Since escalation started, many of them have been mobilized for other tasks; the total is now 130. In all, some 600 people have left the village since 1965, for reasons relating to the general resistance to aggression. Three companies of militia have been made up from the young men and girls of the commune.

Arable land covers an area of 870 maus. The co-operative has a labour force of 1,400. The administrative staff – which also plays an active part in production – has nine members. There is a technical staff of seven (i.e. mechanics and electricians paid by the co-operative) and a team of five agricultural experts.

Prior to 1960, the village was dependent on a single, annual rice crop. The production of rice has increased (see Table 10).

Table 10. Rice production 1959–66.

	Area under cultivation (in maus)	Tons per acre	Quantity of rice produced (in tons)
1959	857	0.409	339.372 (one harvest)
1960	855	0.891	667.900 (two harvests)
1961	850	1.637	1,237.158 (progress against flooding)
1962	849	1.660	1,253.124
1963	849	1.721	1,298.970
1964	845	1.799	1,351.560
1965	838	1.498	1,116.216 (outbreak of yellowing)
1966	810	1.994	1,339.680

In addition, production has been diversified. Jute and sweet potato are now being grown. The two crops are intercalated over an area of thirty-one maus, producing about eighteen hundredweight of jute and four tons of sweet potato per mau. Fish-breeding has been developed.

Income from fish-breeding (in dongs)

1961	27,000
1962	36,000
1963	42,000
1964	57,000
1965	61,000
1966	82,000

Stock farming is not a large factor in the co-operative, for there is a shortage of fodder. Since 1963, fifteen tons of live geese and ducks have been sold to the state each year, at a rate of about 1.09 dongs per pound. The co-operative owns 400 hens, and the chicks they produce are sold to members at the official price. Production of soused shrimps averaged four tons between 1961 and 1963; since then, it has averaged seven. At present, the co-operative is thinking of manufacturing pickle (Nuoc Mam); the expectation is that ten tons could be produced, which would be sold to the state at the official price of about 1,200 dongs a ton.

The co-operative has likewise set about developing handicrafts: the peasants of earlier times used to engage in these, as a sideline. The results are remunerated by the state. Gunny bags earn the co-operative an average of 150,000 dongs a year, and basket-making brings in another 41,000. The combined annual return for brickmaking and lime production is about 60,000 dongs.

About a dozen households make fans, on an independent basis. In 1960, every household owned one pig; in 1965, the average was two pigs; in 1967, 2.5 pigs. From 1961 until 1963, the peasants privately sold the state fourteen tons of poultry a year; the figure for 1965–7 was fifteen tons.

QUOC TRI

Pham Van Ha, aged thirty-six, Party Secretary of the commune, political head of the self-defence platoon:

There weren't any roads in those days, just small muddy tracks on which it was impossible to walk two abreast; there were thick bushes on either side, and you could hardly get by if you were carrying a heavy load of straw. The dry season was the only possible harvest-time. The yield was between eighteen and twenty-two hundredweights. The annual harvest covered our needs for only three or four months. People did not visit one another's houses, for the paths were always eight inches deep in mud. On the other hand, there was no clean water. The village had a kind of pond at either end, and these ponds were referred to as wells. People would often scoop water straight from the paddy-fields; not that it made much difference, as the wells weren't rimmed anyway. There were no water-closets. Everyone used to do it on the paths beside the paddy-fields. Disease was common: typhoid, trachoma, cholera ... In 1943, cholera claimed a hundred victims here in Quoc Tri. The people used to think demons had descended on the village.

Even members of the same family didn't dare visit each other. They all went about armed with machetes, ready to defend themselves against the cholera-demon. Special ceremonies were performed in the hope of appeasing the spirits. In those days, good and bad harvests were attributed to the whims of the guardian spirits. Everyone in my family was illiterate before the revolution.

My family had to leave the village and move to the province of Thai Binh. Many others had to emigrate to new areas, where they set up hamlets – all bearing the particle 'Duong' (for Quoc Tri used to be called Trieu Duong). During the great famine of 1945, there were 447 deaths out of a population of 3,500. A lot of people have left the village since. My own family were landless peasants: all they had was a house and a small yard. They were hired labourers, working for landowners. My father tried to move to another district, but the village elders drove him away: they didn't want outsiders. On another occasion he went off to the highlands to be a woodcutter; but that didn't work out either, so he came back.

I was eleven when my father died, after an illness, at the age of fifty-four. My mother died of starvation during the great famine of 1945. I was fourteen at the time. We were a family of six. The eldest was twenty-five and the youngest nine. My little sister and I took jobs, looking after landowners' children. My sister was in a very poor state of health in those days, due to overwork, but she has since recovered. Today she is a factory-hand at the Thai Nguyen ironworks – which has been bombed, by the way. At that time, I ate one meal a day: rice with fig-leaves, and usually a soup made from rice and bran. There were no vegetables: all we had was rice and salt. One of my sisters died of starvation in 1945; another was killed during a bombardment in 1948. And one of my brothers was killed in the army in 1953. That leaves three of us: the factory-hand, myself and my elder brother, who is secretary of one of the local Party cells – we have sixteen cells in Quoc Tri.

There used to be nine landowners in this village; in the commune as a whole, there were sixty. In those days the 'poor peasant' lived in a hut and slept on a straw mattress. You had to be an 'average peasant' to afford a bamboo bed. Mosquito nets were unheard of. People had very little clothing, and things got even worse during the Japanese occupation: the villagers used to cover their bodies with bits of sacking. 'We have the earth as our bed,' they joked, 'straw as our matting, sacks as our clothing.' It was general practice to grind the rice-husks and mix them with the grains, in an attempt to fill empty stomachs. The landowners used to hold huge feasts and make the villagers contribute. Some of them had three wives. They ate meat or chicken every day. When you were working for them, you got a few sweet potatoes in the morning and some rice at midday. That was for heavy labour. Anyone who didn't tire himself with work was sacked on the spot and would sometimes even forfeit his day's pay; there was no one he could take the matter up with. If they wanted to grab a peasant's land, they would plant some liquor in his home (the colonial administration had exclusive rights to liquor) and tip off the authorities. The peasant was duly prosecuted and had to sell his plot. That is how my uncle was dispossessed. And another thing: peasants would run into debt whenever the taxes fell due. The interest rate was 50 per cent for a period of six months. They would just manage to pay off the interest. The debt itself was never disposed of. In those days, to gain admission to the circle of elders – who enjoyed a special prestige and were looked up to by the rest of the community – you had to pay for a giant feast. I knew some old men who provided such a feast and then committed suicide. Ceremonial funerals were very expensive, and people were often so heavily in debt after burying the head of the family that they had to flee the village. The poorer a family was, the greater the attempts to make it sell its land, fall into debt and move to another part of the country. I was only a small child at the time, but I saw it happen and I shall never forget the experience. My grandfather had three sons. In 1943 the village notables decided to put pressure on my family. At their bidding a man came to my uncle's house, feigned insanity and set fire to the place. Luckily the flames were soon extinguished, but the 'lunatic' had smashed everything in reach. The whole family hurried to the rescue, and the two notables accompanying the 'lunatic' were seized and bound. But my two uncles were arrested for laying hands on the notables. There was pandemonium at the district court. In the end, my uncles had to sell all they owned to pay for the trial and were sentenced to three months' imprisonment. We had already lost three saos as a result of the liquor incident, and now the last four saos had to be sold. We had nothing left. In 1945, the young uncle to whom all this had happened was the first person in Quoc Tri to join the self-defence forces; afterwards, the whole family served in the Resistance.

On 5 August 1945 there was a demonstration in support of the seizure of power. Three hundred villagers marched on the district town, seized the stocks of rice on behalf of the Vietminh, and shared them out. Later, the government called on the population to prepare to resist aggression. The landowners joined in, but it was the peasants who played the most active part and fought with most ardour. My whole family was involved in the war. I was only fourteen, but I was in the Pioneers. The southern part of the province remained a 'free zone'. Between 1945 and 1949, people's organizations were set up and many young men and women recruited. Anyone over eighteen could join the self-defence forces. Some landowners went over to the invader, others behaved like patriots. There were five of these in the two local villages, and today they are still members of the National Front. Four military posts were set up in the commune in 1949, but this did not stop the resistance organizations from taking root and spreading. Hideouts were prepared for the militants. The cadres mostly came at night to train and instruct the population. At that time, there was a municipal council collaborating with the colonial authorities. Taxes and requisitions were being actively fought against. On one occasion they subjected an elderly peasant to the water-torture, filling his stomach with liquid until it reached bursting point. As a reprisal, the Vietminh arrested a member of the puppet council, took him to an area which was in our hands, and forced the council to disband despite the presence of the military posts. These posts were manned by puppet troops under French leadership. There were also a number of North Africans. They combed the entire area in the hope of finding the militants, and they held several hundred people in close confinement. But nobody would talk, and nobody would agree to become village chief in place of the kidnapped man.

Until 1952, there were no serious military engagements round about here – just isolated clashes. Sometimes a platoon of armed partisans would open fire on the enemy troops, who would then proceed to raze the village as a reprisal. Quoc Tri was razed three times. That is why there is no bamboo around the village. We had an intricate system of underground trenches and shelters. By 1953, or thereabouts, the village was completely under our control: they never succeeded in re-establishing the puppet municipal council. It was becoming possible for us to seal off the village. Then they started battering us with artillery and from the air. The commune was hit by something like a thousand shells. Some of the villagers moved out; the rest stayed put and lent support to the partisans. In 1953, the GMs [groupes mobiles] launched operation 'Brochet', which extended to all parts of the region. A regiment tried to besiege the village. One battalion forced its way in, while the other two kept guard outside. The battalion remained in the village for twenty-four hours. On the second night, the partisans emerged from cover and wiped the battalion out. The French artillery opened up – and this, of course, made it impossible for the other two battalions to intervene. Meanwhile we started attacking the posts – which meant that the two battalions had to fall back and get them out of trouble. That was the last time they set foot in Quoc Tri. In March 1954 the Vietminh knocked the two posts out, and after that the village was safe behind our own lines. Our troops went off to fight the enemy in another part of the province.

I had been in the army for five years, having enlisted when I was seventeen. At first I was turned down because I was under-age and under-weight. But I was so insistent (explaining how I wanted to fight in order to avenge my family) that in the end they accepted me. I was in the regular forces, though fighting behind enemy lines in what were known as 'independent units'. De Lattre had constructed his belt of bunkers round the delta, but this didn't stop us from getting men through. I was wounded twice, but each time I returned to active service. In 1951 I took part in our counter-mopping-up operations when the GMs launched operations 'Lemon' and 'Tangerine'. In 1952 we tried to knock out the smaller posts along the rear of de Lattre's lines, in an attempt to liberate the south of Hung Yen province. I also took part in attacks on gunboats stationed along the Luoc; we blasted our way through the lines, swam out to the gunboats and blew them up – they were big craft, carrying nine lifeboats. In 1953 I was awarded the Military Medal. The following year, I fought in the area around Road 5 and afterwards along the south-western fringe of the delta, which was the starting point of the supply lines to Dien Bien Phu. I was demobilized in 1955 and came back to the village. I became deputy leader of the self-defence platoon. I had learned to read and write by then, having completed two classes in the army. After 1955, I completed two more. Now I am at Class 7 standard.

At the time there weren't many people left in the village, but they gradually drifted back. In 1955–6 the land reform programme was carried out:

- Eight hundred and twenty households received 620 maus of land, plus ponds covering a total area of twenty maus.
- Four hundred and eighty households received no grants of land, either because they had received some in 1953, before Dien Bien Phu, or because they already had enough. Instead, they were given houses, furniture or rice.
- Fifty-nine households were stripped of 620 maus. When the mistakes of the land reform programme were set right, five households were rehabilitated and had 6.5 maus restored to them. On average, the land reform programme conferred 1.7 saos per head.

There were public meetings at which people spoke out against the evils of the past, recalling acts of extortion and other crimes perpetrated by the landowners. Forty local landowners fled to the South.

Offending landowners were brought before the assembled crowd in response to the peasants' demands. Two of them were tried and sentenced to terms of imprisonment. The worst offenders had left by that time – there were no executions here. Three landowners had fought in the Resistance, but this did not prevent them from being tried. They were rehabilitated in 1957, for their sons were in the army and they themselves had given shelter to militants. Today they are members of the co-operatives: one is a provincial cadre; the second is a member of the National Front; the third is just an ordinary co-operative worker. At about that time, Vu Manh – who is now Chairman of the Administrative Committee – was accused of belonging to a reactionary organization; this was because he was operating under cover and hardly anyone in the village knew him. Witnesses testified to his loyal activities, but in the pent-up atmosphere of the land reform programme a number of mistakes were made. Vu Manh was jailed, but he never swerved from his belief that the truth would one day be acknowledged. Today he is Deputy Party Secretary and Chairman of the Committee.

After the rectification campaign, mutual-aid teams were set up – each team being made up of about a dozen households. Production capacity was still weak, for irrigation work had not yet begun; there was widespread flooding, and it was impossible to reap more than one harvest a year. The yield in those days was just over fourteen hundredweights per acre. The yield increased, for the peasants were working their own land. In 1959–60 came the second step: a trial co-operative was set up. Sixteen households banded together to form this co-operative, and among them were two Party members. (At the time, there were only sixteen Party members in the entire commune.) The first harvest was not a good one. Nobody had any previous experience of running a co-operative, and the peasants could not be talked into contributing their own plots to the general resources of land. Some peasants claimed that their plots had been confiscated.

The results – and the standards of work – were poor. The yields obtained by the co-operative were lower than those obtained on privately owned land. Nine households asked permission to leave the co-operative. Even the Party members felt that the remainder should be allowed to withdraw if they wished, that the co-operative should then be wound up, and that there was no point in continuing. So then the people in charge met and tried to work out a solution: they must find some way of establishing co-operatives which would genuinely raise the standard of living, or in four or five years' time there would be tremendous inequalities in the rural areas. Public meetings were held. Members of the local Party described what their lives had been like before the revolution. This was known as 'conjuring up the hardships and uncertainties of the past'. Sessions of this kind were arranged whenever people showed signs of doubt and uncertainty; the past was raked over, and because the experience was a collective one the atmosphere soon became charged with emotion – many people cried as they listened to all they had been through. Some of the Party members were rich peasants, and they were prepared to acknowledge that those who had previously been exploited now deserved to be masters of their own land. They insisted that unless we made up our minds to embrace the co-operative system, there would be a general return to the conditions of the past. These words impelled the landless peasants to follow the line laid down by the Party. The families who had been on the point of leaving the co-operative were persuaded to change their minds. Everyone admitted that life had changed completely in the last few years – not only for the people who had acquired land for the very first time, but for those who had been helpless victims of the rich and powerful and who were now rid of the fear of piling up debts. We then moved on to the second stage in the argument. We said: 'If people don't join the co-operative, how can we ever hope to reap two harvests a year? For who will carry out irrigation works?' In the end, only one household still wanted to leave; the other eight agreed to stay. The cadres were unable to persuade the head of the dissident family. 'I shall wait and see how the next few harvests go,' he said, 'and I shall join the co-operative if things improve.' The members of the co-operative then proceeded to build a dikelet four feet high and five eighths of a mile long, which enabled them to reap two harvests a year over an area of seven maus. At the end of the year, nearly all the villagers asked to join the co-operative so that they might share the benefits conferred by two harvests. The man who had left the co-operative refused to be swayed, however; during the rainy season he worked as a fisherman and a pedlar. By late 1959, there were nine small co-operatives making preparations for the summer 1960 harvest; 30 per cent of the peasant households were now members, following the success of the initial co-operative. At the end of 1960, 97 per cent asked to remain within the co-operative, for the summer harvest had been a good one. Naturally, the peasant would rather work his own land; but there is something which means even more to him, and that is the chance to produce more and enjoy better standards of living. In the end-of-the-year harvest of 1960, there was extensive flooding due to immoderately heavy rainfall; part of the expected yield was lost, but some was saved through the collective efforts of the community. There were two types of reaction to this event. There were those who said: 'The harvest has been lost', and those who said: 'Some has been salvaged'. This setback resulted in thirty requests to leave the co-operative and about a hundred waverers.

Once again we organized a meeting. Co-operatives seemed the right idea, but how were we to ensure their success? There must be no loss of heart, least of all among Party members. The question was asked: 'Can any member of the Party allow the people to return to the hardships of the past?' Everyone agreed that the answer must be no. In that case, the present difficulties must be overcome. This was easier said than done, for the mood of discouragement was spreading. Drawing on the experience of the first co-operative, we decided that all co-operatives should be protected with dikes. This was something which had not been done for centuries, but we decided it was a step we must take on behalf of the Party. Securing the commune against floods was a mighty undertaking; but having fought the French and endured so much, we saw no reason why we should not achieve this as well.

Within six months, 700 workers toiling in shifts had built a protective dike ten feet high, four feet wide, and two and a half miles in circumference. (The total area of the commune is

1,070 maus.) There was some opposition to the scheme, especially from former landowners and well-to-do peasants; they went about saying that the venture was doomed to failure, that nothing like it had ever been done before, and that it was a complete waste of time and energy. Doubt took root among the ordinary people. We did our best to fight against defeatism. Food was still in short supply in those days — people were still not getting enough to eat; but this was exactly the reason why the project had to be completed. 'With the Party, you can succeed,' we argued. 'When President Ho said we could beat the French, it seemed impossible; but we did it. Building the dike seems impossible, but we can do that too.' In 1961 the main dike was finished. The following year, we completed work on the externals: dikelets, bridges, penstocks for controlling the water level. We could now be certain of getting two harvests a year. And with these hydraulic problems solved, every effort has been made since 1965 to improve agricultural techniques which will step up production. Irrigation has been rationalized (e.g. the water must be withdrawn once the ears ripen). And the problem of fertilizers is receiving careful attention. Barrow-loads of alluvial deposits are collected from the area beyond the dike; there is a special team in charge of this operation. The commune is now equipped with dual-compartment cesspools. In addition, animal dung and certain other excreta can be used as manure. We give six and a half pounds of rice for every two and a half hundredweights of dung. Since the attacks started, we have continued to do all we can to increase production.

Education

Nguyen Dinh Quy, aged sixty-seven, retired schoolmaster, living in a comfortable house in Quoc Tri with a small, well-kept garden:

I came from a family of poor peasants. I had six brothers, five of whom were illiterate. I was singled out to go to school, while the rest of the family laboured to support me. I studied Chinese characters, and then the Vietnamese language. At sixteen I began to study French and gained my lower certificate of education. Afterwards I spent two years at a teachers' training college in Nam Dinh, where I duly qualified. I secured a post at a district school serving six villages. There was a single classroom in which the children were taught to read, write and count. That was in 1920. There were between fifty and sixty pupils, all from wealthy families. It was no simple matter to acquire even this amount of education: you had to grease the palm of the provincial director of schools and take presents to him four times a year, otherwise he would expel your child. To obtain a place at a teachers' training college you had to pay two and a half piastres a month, and appointments went only to those who were prepared to hand over a fifty-piastre bribe. (My whole family, made up of eleven members, ate only five piastres-worth of rice a month.) I was assigned to the school at Tien Ba, in the district of Quynh Coi (Thai Binh province). I had to return to Hung Yen to pay my respects to the French Resident, and when I arrived at Thai Binh I had to do the same. Respects had also to be paid to the chief mandarin of the province, to the director of education, and to the district chief. In addition, I had to call – bearing suitable gifts – on the head of the canton and on the council of elders. That was the custom. One was subject to a triple hierarchy: the notables, the mandarins, the French. Further presents had to be distributed annually, at the Lunar New Year; and should a superior happen to mention that such-and-such a date was the anniversary of his father's death, one was expected to honour *him* with a present too.

Anyway, there was I with my class of sixty, all children of rich parents. On one of my first days at the school, being entirely without experience, I accepted the son of a town crier. I was duly reprimanded by the head of the canton, who sent for me and said: 'What! Call yourself a schoolmaster, and you can't appreciate the difference between the son of a person of standing and the son of a town crier?' So I had to teach him separately, in my free time.

Whenever there was a communal feast, one had to take offerings to the tutelary spirits. Since this added to my material difficulties, I failed to attend one year; whereupon the head of the canton ordered me to clear out all my desks and benches and lodged a formal complaint with the district and provincial authorities, stating that the schoolmaster did not respect the spirits and must be dismissed. I had to leave the area and go and teach in another part of the country.

In those days one had to teach children of different age-groups and different standards, all in the same classroom. It was very hard work and not at all efficient. The Vietnamese language was pushed into the background, and dictations in Annamese were a rarity. Much emphasis was laid on 'our ancestors, the Gauls'. French was used for teaching mathematics and for telling the moralistic stories which were supposed to improve the pupils' characters.

Some schoolteachers were quite content to spend their time playing cards, sipping China tea or smoking opium. Some were ambitious and tried to become mandarins. Some were aware of our subjection, were ashamed of being slaves, and taught from a sense of patriotism; many of these soon became under-cover agents for the Party.

This was already a well-populated region, but there was little rice and it was possible to bring in only one harvest a year. Capitation taxes were levied annually. The head of the canton, or the elders, used to come round with the cards, charging 2.5 piastres for a fifty-sous green card and five piastres for a 2.5 red card. Those who did not pay on demand were seized and bound; their fingers and legs were cruelly compressed in clamps and vices, and they were beaten. It cost the officials a great deal merely to keep their administrative machinery in operation – for although they produced nothing, they were heavy consumers. Police used to come and take away the poultry and furniture of those who were unable to pay; and at ploughing time they would confiscate the buffaloes, so that families had to work the ploughs themselves. The landowners took every advantage of these opportunities to add to their wealth. They lent money at high rates of interest to enable people to settle their existing debts; many peasants would be unable to repay the loan, and the landowners would then take possession of their plots and homes. Nearly everyone was downtrodden. If you were born poor, you stayed poor and often grew poorer and poorer. For a large part of the year, most people lived on what little they made from the sale of rice. They wore loin-cloths because those were the best garments for wading, and they had nothing else. There used to be a song containing the words: 'We have spent our lives wading, and our bones will still be sodden after death.'

FIRST AND SECOND PHASES (QUOC TRI)

There are 1,500 pupils and a teaching staff of thirty-nine in the community of 4,400 inhabitants.

Infant classes	280 children	6 staff members
First phase	720 pupils	15 teachers
Second phase	500 pupils	18 fully qualified masters and mistresses

At the time of my visit, only one class was being taught in the huge, solidly constructed building: the rest of the school had been split up and sent elsewhere in the interests of safety. The forty boys and girls stood up politely as we entered the room. There were trenches running along the central aisle and beneath the wooden forms; pupils occupying the middle of these forms had to straddle their legs for support.

Five young masters and mistresses were on the premises. Four are the sons or daughters of poor peasants; the fifth is the son of a skilled craftsman. Three are natives of the village, and the other two are from homes elsewhere in the district. All of them have completed seven classes of general education and spent two years at a teachers' training college.

The pupils taking the first-phase course are aged between seven and eleven. This course lasts four years. Previously there were a number of older pupils who had missed early schooling for one reason or another, but this situation has since been remedied. All seven-year-old children in the commune are now receiving full-time education. Classes are timed to last between thirty and forty-five minutes, according to age. The syllabus is as follows:

Arithmetic: Addition, subtraction, multiplication, division, whole numbers, decimals, the metric system, weights and measures, how to reckon time and speed, areas (in maus and saos), the rule of three.

Geometry: Surfaces – squares, circles, parallelograms . . .

Science: General ideas about soil, cultivation, stock-farming, water, irrigation and drainage problems. These general ideas are illustrated by practical work on the school allotment.

Language: Grammar, reading, composition. By the end of the course, pupils are capable of providing written descriptions of objects, scenes, feelings.

Geography: The course is centred on the DRV itself. The children are also taught about countries which have close ties with Vietnam: China, Laos, Cambodia, the Soviet Union.

History: After listening to stories about national heroes, pupils study the main periods in the country's history up to 1954, with special attention to the present era.

The mornings are devoted to lessons. In the afternoons, the children help their families.

The second-phase course lasts three years and is for pupils between the ages of eleven and fourteen. The syllabus for this group is:

Mathematics: Simple equations.

Physics: Optics, electricity, heat.

Chemistry: Basics of inorganic chemistry.

Natural science: Evolution of the species (Darwin).

Literature: Vietnamese classics from the thirteenth century to the present day, with special emphasis on contemporary authors. Until recently, extracts from the works of foreign writers were studied (e.g. Gorky and Lu Hsün), but these are now held over until the third phase.

Languages: No foreign languages are taught at this stage.

Geography: General geography, physical geography, local geography.

History: History of Vietnam, from early times to the present. A few sessions are devoted to world history (e.g. the October Revolution and the Chinese revolution of 1949) as a background to the history of modern Vietnam.

The second-phase course also includes classes in agricultural technology. Pupils study the soil, seeds, irrigation and drainage problems, the use of fertilizers and insecticides, stock-farming, fish-breeding, etc. Practical work is carried out on the land belonging to the school: three saos of paddy-fields and two saos of dry land. As soon as their schooling is over, the young people place themselves at the disposal of the co-operative; the teachers tell the officials in charge exactly what training their pupils have received so that maximum use may be made of their talents. In 1966, seventy pupils completed their second-phase education. Thirty-five moved on to the third phase; twenty enrolled at agricultural training schools; ten joined co-operatives. A few took a special eighth-year course while awaiting call-up. Generally speaking, jobs demanding particular care are nowadays entrusted to the young, for the co-operatives have come to realize that their technical standards are distinctly higher.

There has been no reduction of syllabuses since the escalation of the war. To make up for time lost through the disruption of classes, however, a great effort has been made to concentrate on essentials in each subject.

In 1967, the commune was educating seventy more pupils than in the previous year. Trenches were dug early in 1966 – the work being carried out by the co-operative. There has been a discernible change in standards of work since the air raids started: pupils are now studying harder and better.

One of the teachers told me:

In October 1966, the Americans bombed a school at Tauy Dom, in the neighbouring province of Thai Binh. Thirty children were killed. The pupils at the school in Quoc Tri were assembled and informed of the news: it roused them to hatred against the aggressors. They began to exert themselves more – those who used to be absent a great deal now attend regularly. Since then, the Americans have bombed the schools at Huong Phuc, in the province of Ha Tinh, and Hai Hoa, in the province of Thanh Hoa. On each occasion, we told the pupils about it. In addition to strictly academic subjects, they study the lives and deaths of heroes like Nguyen Van Troi.

The task of liberating the South is a topic of daily discussion. The distance from Hanoi to Saigon is 1,700 kilometres. The pupils who do the best work are awarded a hundred points, equivalent to kilometres. The one who receives most points is the first to enter Saigon.

Anybody who gets ten out of ten in a test is supposed to have shot down a plane; anybody who gets eight is supposed to have captured an American airman. We also have exhibitions of photographs dealing with the war in the North and South, and these are kept scrupulously up to date. There are debates on the subject of the South, and competitions to see who can collect most news from the press and radio about our victories or American outrages: the prize goes to whoever gives the best account of these events in the current affairs class. This scheme operates chiefly among the second-phase pupils.

In addition to coping with the problems raised by present-day events, we try to feed the children's curiosity about the fighting traditions of the nation and of the province. We display weapons and trophies dating from the first war of resistance. We invite men and women who fought in that war to come along and describe what it was like; alternatively, we invite the families of those who laid down their lives. And, to assist in ideological training, we have also built up a small museum containing the rags which the poor peasants wore as clothing in the old days, together with typical contracts referring to debts and seizures of land. Items formerly belonging to mandarins are on show too. Such objects provide perfect illustrations of the social background to some of the books the pupils study – e.g. *Quand la lampe s'éteint*[2].

At the end of their seventh year, many are eager to join the army; some even lie about their age or their weight, in the hope of being accepted for service. While still studying, the older pupils help with the agricultural work; on average, they earn a quarter of the points usually earned by an adult. Sometimes there are periods of what is known as 'socialist labour' – repairing roads or improving the irrigation and drainage system. All pupils are assigned to these tasks, and so are the teaching staff.

Over the years, there has been a steady improvement in courses. Previously, there was a tendency to follow Soviet syllabuses too closely: children were taught about bears instead of buffaloes, about birches instead of banana trees.

We are also doing our best to condense lessons, in case the war should become more severe. It is no easy task to reduce a forty-five-minute lesson to half an hour without omitting anything of value; but such cuts will enable us to go on teaching whatever the difficulties.

First-phase teachers are paid thirty-five to forty dongs, second-phase teachers forty to forty-five dongs. The pay is just high enough for a married couple to bring up one child,

2. *Quand la lampe s'éteint* by Ngo Tat To, translated into French by Le Lien Vu and Georges Boudarel, Foreign Languages Publishing House, Hanoi, 1959. This novel describes peasant life in the delta during the days of colonial rule.

or at a pinch two. A single person has to save for two years before he or she can afford a bicycle. (Admittedly, cycles are very expensive – 275 dongs.) As for accommodation, twenty teachers live in their own homes within the commune. The remainder lodge together and share an allotment. We don't pay any rent; we *do* pay for our meals, but the cook receives her wages from the local authority. Food costs eighteen dongs a month – less if the allotment is producing well. We are allowed five and a half yards of clothing materials a year. For the rest, we often send a little money home to our families. We buy books and newspapers. We devote some of our spare time to do-it-yourself tasks, producing whatever materials we are short of: we draw our own maps, for instance. What do we lack? A more advanced general culture, a higher political standard. Apart from that, I think the women teachers would like more clothes. And we should all like transistor radios. Our requirements are modest, you see. The war has reduced everything to simple terms.

A THIRD-PHASE SCHOOL (HUNG YEN PROVINCE)

For security reasons, the school is based in a small village. There are nine others in the province. This is the oldest third-phase school in Hung Yen. The third phase is the highest level of pre-university general education. The classes are numbered 8, 9 and 10 (there are five of each), and the pupils are aged between fourteen or fifteen and seventeen or eighteen. There is a teaching staff of fifty-four, including nine young women, to deal with 635 pupils.

In 1966, 134 pupils left the school; fifty-four of them were girls. They all went on to the university, apart from five who joined the army. Without exception, the students are the sons and daughters of peasants – usually poor peasants. The masters and mistresses are local people too, apart from a few who have been transferred from Hanoi. All of them have spent ten years at school and three more at an advanced teachers' training college; in addition, all of them have taken special courses in agriculture, hydraulic engineering, etc. The majority are between twenty-three and thirty; the oldest are thirty-five. Their monthly salary is between fifty-five and sixty-five dongs. The school is considered one of the best and most advanced in North Vietnam.

When the school was evacuated here, the staff's first act was to make a tour of the neighbouring villages so that their teaching methods might take full account of the needs and potentialities of the local population. They were anxious to obtain the support of the families and Administrative Committees in the area, for only with their help could they give the pupils a complete and properly co-ordinated training.

This year, all the villages in the area have played their part in digging the school trenches. Peasants have lent plots of land for use in agricultural experiments. The villagers have welcomed the pupils to their allotments and taught them how to perform grafts. The students are engaged in productive work in the afternoons. To rate as a good student, you have to do well on the land as well: at the end of each month, the school requires each pupil to produce a certificate from his co-operative indicating the quality of his work. The staff are doing their best to train people who will be not only competent academics but able technicians too. Many of the students repair machinery in their villages. Others are experts on seeds, insecticides, grafting . . .

In addition, the school provides political education, PT classes and, with assistance from the army authorities, military training (rifle-shooting, passive defence, marching, etc.). Each class is organized as a platoon, and manoeuvres are held. Many students receive medical training. On 9 September 1967, following an air raid less than a mile away, a dozen casualties were given first aid by pupils of the school.

As well as attending current affairs classes dealing with the progress of the war, developments in the South, and so on, students are instructed in the fundamentals of Marxism-Leninism (Class 9) and in the successive phases of the Vietnamese revolution (Class 10). Among other subjects tackled are: modes of production; the problems confronting state and Party; imperialism and its role; historical materialism.

In natural science lessons, experimental graftings are carried out. And by their final year pupils are studying differential co-efficients, atomic theory, semiconductors, polymers, the rudiments of cosmology, and the general laws of genetics: Mendel, Morgan, Lysenko, Michurin[3]. In literature, the main emphasis is on Vietnamese authors, but other literatures are dealt with as well. One foreign language is taught – either Russian or Chinese – and the students read works by Tolstoy, Ostrovsky, Pushkin, Lermontov, Gorky, Victor Hugo, Balzac, Molière, Shakespeare, Lu Hsün and the poets of the Tang dynasty.

Less attention is paid to physical geography (already taught in the second-phase schools) than to economic geography. Lessons in this subject relate to Vietnam, the major powers (the Soviet Union, the United States, Germany, Japan, France, Great Britain, China) and the countries of South-east Asia. Cuba and the other socialist states are studied too.

Here is the history syllabus, as an indication of the general standard:

Class 8: Early times to the present day. 'Primitive' societies. Egypt, China, Greece, Rome. The European Middle Ages. The Chinese Middle Ages. The Renaissance. The bourgeois-democratic revolutions in Britain and France. Utopian and scientific socialism. The struggles of the working classes in Europe. 1848. The Commune. The colonial invasion of Asia and Africa.

Class 9: Contemporary history. The First World War. The history of Vietnam from the French invasion to 1918.

3. This syllabus may be revised in the near future.

The October Revolution. The world since the October Revolution. The capitalist world after the First World War. The building of socialism in the USSR. The world revolution after 1917. The crisis of 1929. The rise of Fascism. The Second World War. The world after 1945. The movements of national liberation. The capitalist world after 1945. The socialist world since 1945. The Chinese revolution.

Class 10: Vietnam from 1918 to 1950.

Class 8 examines the economic geography of the capitalist countries, and Class 9 deals with the economic geography of the socialist countries, excluding Vietnam. Class 10 focuses its attention on Vietnam itself, and also the province of Hung Yen. Indeed, each pupil is required to make a study of a given field of activity in a given locality and draw up a programme showing how that activity can be developed. Groups of ten or a dozen pupils are sent to a commune for a period of two to four weeks and have to write a monograph on the area, evaluating the situation and proposing solutions to any short-comings.

In literature, Class 8 devotes four hours a week during the first term to popular Vietnamese writings, and four hours a week during the second term to the popular theatre from the eleventh century to the eighteenth century, with special attention to Nguyen Trai.

Class 9 moves on to foreign literature: the *Iliad*, Chinese legends and tales, *l'Avare* by Molière. Lessons are also devoted to eighteenth- and nineteenth-century Vietnamese literature, with special attention to the *Kieu* and to the historical chronicle of this period, the *Chinh Phu Ngam* ('The Lament of the Warrior's Wife'). The second half of the year is given over to Vietnamese literature from 1859 to 1930: patriotic writings, realism, etc., plus a few texts by fellow-travellers. In foreign literature, the students are introduced to Balzac's *Eugénie Grandet*, Tolstoy's *War and Peace*, and the tales of Hsün Sin.

Class 10 studies Vietnamese literature from 1930 onwards: patriotic and revolutionary poems, and the various trends in realism. The selected foreign texts are: Gorky's *Mother*, Ostrovsky's *And The Steel Was Tempered*, and the poems of Mayakovsky.

This syllabus applies to the whole country.

The staff encourage students to keep diaries and collect the folktales, proverbs and songs of the surrounding countryside. Before the bombing started, poets and other writers used to be invited to the school. Every effort is made to foster an active interest in literature.

There are lessons every morning from 7 a.m. till 11.30 a.m. The pupils work on the land every afternoon during the first half of the year; but the second half is devoted entirely to schoolwork.

The timetable for students in their final year is as follows: mathematics, six hours; literature, four hours; foreign languages, two hours; physics, five hours; history, an hour and a half; chemistry, three hours; biology, two hours; agricultural technology, two hours; geography, an hour and a half; politics, an hour and a half; current affairs, thirty minutes; PT and military training, two hours; music, one hour; industrial work, sixteen three-hour sessions per year (devoted, say, to theoretical and practical study of the internal combustion engine).

There is talk of a general remoulding of syllabuses to allow for the growing importance which the exact sciences are assuming. Subjects like Euclidean geometry, for instance, may be dropped so that more time and energy shall be available for items which seem of greater value in the present scientific context. This matter is being carefully explored, in spite of the war.

THE AGRICULTURAL TRAINING SCHOOL AT TO HIEU

The school was founded in 1963, but the primitive buildings which housed it at first have since been vacated. Early in 1966, it was attractively reconstructed by teams of students enjoying a break from their usual work. It trains junior technicians for the co-operatives of Hung Yen and includes a veterinary centre, a seed-research centre and an artificial insemination centre. Eighty-five acres of land are given over to experiment. The school grounds extend over an area of approximately a third of a square mile.

There are two-year courses for technicians and three-year courses for managerial staff. There are also correspondence courses for people who are already working full-time; these extra-mural students – usually political and administrative cadres – attend classes on two days a month. The pupils are recruited from among officials – and outstandingly good workers – in the co-operatives. Preference is given to the young.

Ten years ago the province had no agricultural experts at all, and only four junior technicians; today it has thirty-five experts and 600 technicians. By 1970, if everything goes according to plan, each co-operative will have three technicians – one dealing with cultivation, one with stock-farming, one with fish-breeding – and two officials of managerial standing. The co-operatives will be reconstituted in larger units, and the expectation is that there will be about 1,000 extra technicians and 1,500 extra managers.

The students, generally aged between eighteen and twenty-three, are required to have completed at least five years' general education; those already holding positions of responsibility may well be older. The total number of students, including correspondence courses, is about 800. There are 270 trainee technicians (including 180 girls), 306 trainee managers (including 210 girls), and 120 correspondence-course students (including eighty women). The school has a teaching staff of thirty-four; of these, a dozen are agricultural experts. All members of the staff possess considerable experience and sound academic qualifications. Four groups of students, totalling 550, have emerged fully trained since 1963. The vast majority are now working in co-operatives; fifty-six of them have taken official posts with the provincial authorities; ten have embarked on courses at the Advanced Agricultural College.

For technical students, the curriculum includes seven months of general education: literature and mathematics (seventh-year level); physics, chemistry, biology and zoology (tenth-year level); economics and politics (to a fairly high standard). After this, they concentrate on a special subject – stock-farming, fish-breeding, etc. The managerial course does not include a special subject; instead, the students study the latest techniques of management and take political courses as well. Each session of theoretical work is followed by a session of practical work.

Subsequently, the students spend a six-month probationary period in a co-operative, where they assist in organizing labour and managing the financial affairs; they also play a direct part in production.

The trainee technicians spend their spell of probation dealing with particular commodities: rice, potatoes, etc. Ninety-five co-operatives (out of a total of 470 in Hung Yen) have taken in parties of students, and in 1966 they all achieved yields of about two and a half tons of rice per acre. The probationers are subsidized by the school, so they are not dependent on the co-operatives. The first batch of newly qualified managerial personnel – 120 students – began full-time work in co-operatives at the end of 1966, and the overall results of those co-operatives are regarded as having improved.

After this period of probation, both groups of students –

technical and managerial – are required to submit an end-of-course thesis. The subject is chosen after consultation with the instructors. The thesis is submitted to a panel of instructors and read out before the author's colleagues and contemporaries. One student at the school wrote a thesis on atrophy in young pigs, and this was commended by the Agricultural Research Institute in Hanoi for its scientific soundness. The teaching staff also undertakes research, in collaboration with other centres.

Qualified personnel working for the co-operatives are paid according to a points system. They are allotted 65 per cent of the top wage in the co-operative, and it is up to them to earn extra points by making an active contribution to production. Like the other workers, they are entitled to cultivate a small private allotment. Technicians are not allowed to earn more than 15 per cent more than the highest-paid worker in the co-operative.

During their studies, the pupils do part-time work to earn their keep. In addition, the co-operatives buy the crops and other items produced at the school. The agricultural experts on the staff are paid seventy dongs a month, and the technicians fifty dongs. The starting capital was put up by the state – 150,000 dongs for the buildings and 350,000 for the fittings and equipment. The land used to be part of a French concession. The state provides a maintenance grant of twenty dongs per pupil per month, and it also pays the teaching staff. The school meets its production costs by borrowing from the provincial bank; it repays the loan in the course of the following year. Twenty per cent of the initial state investment has been repaid in the first four years.

The school is also a test centre for the entire province, demonstrating how the national plan for agricultural development can best be put into effect. It produces about two tons an acre – not per year but per harvest. In the spring 1967 harvest, rice yielded 2.3 tons an acre, maize 1.9, sweet potato

12.5, jute 1.4. There is a nursery planted with longans and orange trees.

Pigs and fish are bred in considerable quantities, and the breeders are sold back to the members of the co-operative.

The school has a small agricultural museum containing prize examples of local produce. Just inside the main entrance are a photograph of Che Guevara, a copy of his famous message ('Two, three, several Vietnams must be created'), and a Cuban book describing the opening session of the Russell Tribunal.

The Work of an Administrative Committee

The commune has 4,100 inhabitants. Administratively, it is made up of four villages operating three co-operatives: a total of 500 maus of paddy-fields and 700 maus of dry cropland. There are 115 Catholics living in these villages; instead of being clustered together, in the usual manner of Catholic families in North Vietnam, the thirty-one households are widely scattered. There is a church, but no parish priest: the congregation is too small. There is also a pagoda, with a Buddhist mo: k and three Buddhist nuns, who work as fully paid members of the co-operative. The older peasants attend the pagoda, but seldom give donations.

The People's Council is made up of fifteen men and fifteen women, all elected by the local population. This People's Council in turn elects nine of its members – five men and four women – to the Administrative Committee. In the village of Xich Dang, six members of the Administrative Committee are also members of the Workers' Party. There is a chairman, two vice-chairmen, and six officials dealing respectively with hydraulic engineering, social concerns, security, culture and ideology, agriculture, military matters. (The official in charge of military matters is also head of the village militia.) They are elected for two years, like the People's Council. Villagers must be over eighteen to vote and over twenty-one to stand for election.

The prime task of an Administrative Committee is to expound the policies of the central government. These are studied in concert with the People's Council, which is responsible for passing them on to the rest of the community.

Every three months the representatives of the People's Council report to the Administrative Council on how things are going in the village; the suggestions, requests and criticisms of local citizens are tabulated and passed on to the district and provincial authorities. Thus there is a continuous flow of communication from top to bottom and bottom to top.

The Administrative Committee is responsible for collecting taxes, marketing produce, and registering births, deaths and marriages. It also initiates publicity campaigns. The current campaign is about the contribution which members of the co-operative are being urged to make against American aggression; the emphasis, of course, is on increased production. Recently, there was a campaign to win acceptance for the new marriage laws, with their insistence on monogamy and equal rights for women. Every effort is made to open people's minds to the wisdom of a law before it is promulgated. The present legislation on matrimony is primarily concerned with avoiding immoderately early marriages, which are frequent in rural areas. Today the minimum age is eighteen for a girl and twenty for a man. There is a judicial board dealing with various lawsuits, most of which are concerned with divorce. Since the new measures were introduced, many women who were once forced into marriage at the age of thirteen or fourteen have begun to seek divorces. The judicial board examines these cases and lays them before the district court for final settlement. In 1966, there were half a dozen divorces.

The Administrative Committee also has a security board, which keeps watch over any elements which the Committee may consider politically unreliable (former landowners, etc.). In Xich Dang, this board has not needed to take active steps in recent years. The cultural affairs board deals with such things as school building and school attendance. In the commune, there are nine crèches, four nursery schools (100 children) and five infant classes (200 pupils). Eight hundred and fifty children are receiving first-phase education, 350 second-phase. There is a teaching staff of twenty-nine. Educational supplies are paid for out of the commune's income, and the state allows a tax refund for this purpose. The schools are built by the local population, and, since the air raids started, the work of digging trenches and erecting shelters has been carried out by the pupils' families. There are two film shows a month, and each co-operative has an arts group – made up principally of young people – which puts on classical plays.

There are two boards – one of eleven members, at commune level, and the other of seven members, at co-operative level – for fostering interest in science and technology; a weekly newspaper on the subject is distributed in every village.

I was assured there had been a considerable advance in mental attitudes:

There are no vagrants nowadays. The old 'soothsayers' work for their living, as do the Buddhist monks. Indeed, this village played an active part in the first war of resistance: the last of the 'soothsayers' had given up practising by 1955. As for the spirit that is supposed to watch over the village, anyone who wishes to pay homage to it is free to do so; few people bother, except the old. Since 1957 there has been no more talk of the guardian dragon objecting to wells being dug, and villagers are no longer sent into trances at ritualistic ceremonies designed to ward off diseases.

Since 1965, the Administrative Committee[4] has been campaigning hard in favour of birth control; in 1966, six sterilizing operations were performed. In this field, matters are still at the experimental stage.

Finally, the Administrative Committee is responsible for

4. The Party Committee takes general decisions, while the Administrative Committee is responsible for carrying out agreed lines of action. There are about a hundred Party members in the commune, and they elect the fifteen officers of the Party Committee. About 30 per cent of the Party members are women in their twenties. The men are older, often belonging to the generation which fought in the first war of resistance.

implementing the local production plan, after consultation with members of the co-operative. And if supply problems arise (e.g. shortage of chemical products), it is the Committee's job to solve them.

Stepping up production is the chief problem at present. Today the work calls for one labourer per mau. The Committee's target is one labourer per two and a half acres – i.e. a threefold increase in productivity. The Committee is pinning its hopes on electrification, mechanization, and improved technical standards among the workers. Electricity has already been installed in one of the four villages, where it is used solely for production purposes. The other villages have diesel engines.

The chairman of the Administrative Committee receives twenty-three dongs a month from the state. In 1966, he did thirty days' extra work in the fields, which earned him 300 points.

Everything has been more straightforward since the air attacks started: labour is easier to mobilize. In the old days, there used to be recalcitrant elements who shirked paying taxes and selling on the official market. There were some who waited for the Lunar New Year and then sold to the highest bidder: they would be hauled before the Administrative Committee, promise to mend their ways, and proceed to do the same thing all over again. But since escalation began, the co-operators themselves have clamped down on these offenders, and the habit is now far less common.

The Organization of a Co-operative

The co-operative is made up of 450 households – 1,925 human beings, including 600 co-operators who are referred to as the 'main labour force' and fifty-four who are termed 'auxiliary labour'. Most of the second group are children or old men. The arable lands cover an area of 450 maus.

When it was founded in 1959, the co-operative comprised only thirty-two households and thirty-one maus of land. A single harvest was all that could be hoped for. By the following year, there was talk of two harvests.

Table 11.

Year	Number of households	Area (in maus)	Rice production (in tons)
1960	82	82	98,668
1961	332	390	572,890
1962	357	417	662,863
1963	368	426	537,778
1964	387	429	677,872
1965	420	450	709,731
1966	438	450	689,300
1967	450	450	—

The 450 maus are made up as follows:

Nurseries: 44 maus (for rice)
Dry crops: 35 maus (sweet potato)
Pig breeding: 26.5 maus
Fruit trees and timber: 4.5 maus
Paddy-fields: 340 maus

Each worker has 7.1 saos to cultivate, and the total area works out at 2.8 saos per head of population.

Organization of labour

There are nine gangs engaged in active production, one gang working in the nurseries (seed selection) and six specialist teams.

Each gang consists of about sixty workers. The specialist teams are smaller: tree planting (25), stock-farming (45), machinery work (9), nurseries (19), fish-breeding (4), brick-making (22), hydraulic engineering (25).

Installations

Four drying floors, covering an area of eight saos, have been built since 1965. So have a piggery containing thirty-three sties (each with room for seven pigs) and seven buffalo sheds (there are forty-six buffaloes and six oxen).

The co-operative has three warehouses, a mechanized husking department, an internal combustion engine, and a fodder-grinding machine.

There are three school buildings, a crèche and nursery run by a permanent staff of eight, and an infirmary with a midwife and male orderly in attendance.

The farming year

The summer rice is sown in October, planted out in January, harvested in May and June. The spring rice is sown in January, planted out in February, harvested in May–June. These are short-term variations. The autumn rice is sown in April, planted out in May, harvested in August. The so-called 'tenth-month' rice (reckoning in lunar months) is sown in April, planted out in June, harvested in November. The co-operative has adopted two new varieties of rice which allow three harvests to be reaped. In 1966, the yield per acre was 1.7 tons. Sweet potato is planted in November and harvested in June. The co-operative devotes only one mau of land to vegetables, for the private allotments are sufficient to meet family needs.

Method of remuneration

Remuneration is assessed by a points system. Generally speaking, every working day is equivalent to ten points. But reference is also made to a scale based on the amount of work performed per mau, and to a daily scale relating to different types of work.

Points scale

Remuneration per task per mau

Nurseries (young rice plants)	25 points
Ploughing, digging	180 points
Harrowing	80 points
Manure haulage	65 points (per 3,500 kilos)
Lifting young rice plants (for pricking out)	180 points
Weeding	210 points
Making dikelets	20 points
Bailing out	50 points
Growing duckweed	210 points
Crop protection and combating insects	15 points
Harvesting	145 points
Minding a buffalo (yearly)	118 points
Helping in a crèche (yearly)	240 points
Helping in a nursery (yearly)	250 points

Scale per working day

Grade 1	Sweeping yards, feeding pigs	6 points
Grade 2	Draining off water, making baskets, etc.	7 points
Grade 3	Hoeing and weeding food crops, fishing, etc.	8 points
Grade 4	Digging, bailing out water, minding a herd of oxen or buffaloes	9 points

Grade 5   Ploughing, harrowing, planting out,
           manuring, clearing, lifting water
           with a blade-wheel, etc.   10 points

The household achieving the highest number of points in
the co-operative notched up 6,480; this was a family of four,
including two full-time workers. The household achieving the
lowest (1,830) consisted of two women: an elderly mother
and her daughter, who was still breast-feeding her child.
Workers qualified in hydraulic engineering completed an
average of 485 working days in 1966 – 4,850 points. Households containing two workers generally attained between three
and four thousand points. The household of the head of the
co-operative attained 4,560.

Domestic economy

Two active workers, each putting in 200 working days, would
achieve 4,000 points. These 4,000 points would qualify the
household for just over twenty-six hundredweights of rice. In
addition, the family is entitled to a share of the proceeds from
the co-operative's fish sales – a share calculated on the basis
of its points. The private allotment (usually about fifteen
saos – 430 square yards) provides sufficient fruit and vegetables
for home consumption, together with a surplus, the bulk of
which is sold to the state and the remainder on the free
market. This surplus generally brings in between 100 and 600
dongs – though some families with especially good fruit trees
manage to earn up to 2,000 dongs. Finally, private stock-
farming (pigs and poultry) usually raises between 150 and
200 dongs.

In this co-operative, which is rather above average, there
are 300 houses built of stone, including 120 with tiled roofs,
and 150 built of cob. All of them have a threshing floor and a
water tank. There are 375 septic tanks, ten family wells and
eight collective wells. Two hundred households have loud-

speakers relaying music and news (cost: twenty-five dongs).
There are forty-five bicycles and ten transistor radios in the
village.

Management

The co-operative assembly consists of 644 workers, who elect
sixty-five representatives. These representatives in turn elect
a Management Committee of seventeen members: a chairman,
two vice-chairmen, the heads of the nine production gangs,
the experts in charge of the specialist teams, an accountant
and a cultural spokesman. There are three women on the
Management Committee, and twelve Party members. (The
co-operative contains forty Party members in all.) The co-
operators reserve the right to dismiss any member of the
Committee before the end of his term of office; this happened
in 1963, on grounds of maladministration. The Committee of
Management meets twice a month to discuss the organization
of labour and implement the production plan, which has been
worked out under the supervision of the commune's Administrative Committee and submitted to the whole co-operative
assembly for amendment.

Accounts

Table 12. Sales to the state (in dongs).

Rice (689 tons)	36,180
Livestock	13,836
Fish	10,025
Bricks	20,785
Fruit	12,572
	93,398

Taxes and hydraulic engineering costs paid to the state:
81,221 tons of rice (monetary value: 21,929 dongs).
The co-operative retained the following:

Seeds	16 tons of rice
Social fund (mutual aid, etc.)	15,486 tons (monetary value: 3,339 dongs)

462,049 tons of rice were shared out among the 450 households in the co-operative according to the number of points each family earned. If some households do not have enough rice (through sickness or short-handedness), the Management Committee sees to it that certain members of the co-operative sell them their surplus – not at the free-market price (2.20 dongs per kilo) but at the state-controlled price (0.27 dongs per kilo). A feeling of solidarity is thereby established among the co-operators. These efforts to achieve a reasonable balance are always conducted in public.

Table 13. Expenses.

Chemical fertilizers	20,697
Pig manure	18,900
Seeds	4,858
Stock-breeding	12,400
Brickmaking	11,668
Fish	3,244
Managerial costs	432
Repayment of loans	4,523
Repairs and sundries	896
	77,618 dongs

In 1966, the co-operative made cash deposits totalling 15,680 dongs with the district branch of the State Bank.

A District Hospital

DISTRICT OF AN THI

This hospital (of fifty beds) was decentralized early in 1966 and is now housed in a series of small, cob-walled buildings. It is run by a surgeon, assisted by sixteen medical auxiliaries – including eight women. It deals only with serious cases and has to cover the needs of 95,000 inhabitants. In all, including orderlies, there is a staff of forty. The hospital has departments dealing with general medicine, surgery, paediatrics and ear, nose and throat complaints. It contains a maternity ward, a laboratory and an X-ray unit.

Once a week, most of the staff go out into the villages and visit the sick at the local treatment centres. The district hospital carries out emergency operations in the following fields: obstetrics, appendicitis, gastric ulcers, rupturing of the spleen or liver, amputations, and all war wounds apart from those involving the chest, lungs and heart (which have to be dealt with at the provincial hospital). Even the orderlies are capable of administering anti-shock injections; the dry plasma employed for this purpose is supplied by the Japanese.

The hospital is responsible for vaccinations and disease prevention throughout the district. Smallpox, diphtheria and typhoid are things of the past, though there are still a few cases of poliomyelitis. Chancre is extremely rare; and so, generally speaking, are all other forms of VD. On the other hand, new diseases have appeared: hypertension and nervous depression resulting from war. Since escalation began, laboratory work has been extended to include forms of analysis previously carried out at the provincial hospital – e.g. functional exploration of the liver, and analysis of the blood and urine. Similarly, the ear, nose and throat department now carries out operations for which patients had, until recently, to travel to Hanoi – for instance, the removal of tonsils and adenoids. There is a practitioner of traditional medicine, who has a special garden for growing the medicinal herbs of the Vietnamese pharmacopoeia. He treats fractures and rheumatic pains, and practises acupuncture.

Traditional medicine

There is a practitioner of traditional medicine in the commune, working for the district hospital and paid by the state. In all, some 15,000 doctors and apothecaries practise this form of treatment; about 10,000 of them are members of the Society of Traditional Medicine. There used to be an Institute of Traditional Medicine in Hanoi, but this has now been disbanded. A thousand rural communes employ practitioners, who are paid by the state.

Each practitioner has a garden for growing medicinal plants. The two methods of treatment are not employed concurrently, for the medicaments have the same basic ingredients. In traditional medicine, rheumatism is treated with Phong Te Thap (in lieu of hydrocortisone). Voi-voi-Bo cong Rnh has the same properties as penicillin, and so has a plant extract known as 'Saidat'. Dysentery is treated with tisanes made from Mo, a plant containing emithine, and diarrhoea with the buds of goyavier leaves or of a plant known as Sim. Committees of inquiry set up by the Faculty of Medicine in Hanoi have also established the success of traditional medicine in combating enteritis, whooping cough and piles. Acupuncturing is extremely effective against convulsions and facial paralysis. After a fracture has been treated with herbs, the damaged limb is held in place by bamboo splints, and the ligaments regain their suppleness in less time than if plaster had been used.

The surgeon in charge of the hospital is a graduate of

Hanoi University, where he spent six years. The medical auxiliaries have completed three-year courses. Since escalation began, they have all learned to act as assistant surgeons and can remove an appendix if the need arises. In cases of emergency, some orderlies are capable of doing the same at the village treatment centres. With conditions as they are at present, the aim is to teach the medical auxiliaries – and indeed the entire medical staff – to perform the widest possible range of tasks with maximum expertise.

The thatched-roof operating theatre has been lined throughout with an American parachute, to avoid dust. The operations performed in October 1967, according to the register, were: forearm fracture, appendicitis, Caesarian, gallstone, ovarian cyst, various amputations due to air raids (four cases), stomach ulcer, obstruction, intestinal invagination, sterilization.

The general standards of health in the district are regarded as satisfactory. There were 196 cases of leprosy in 1960; there has been none since. After the raid on the leper hospital at Quinh Cap (1965), three lepers returned to the district; isolated houses were built for them, and they are now treated at home.

Information about birth control is dispersed by a special committee for the protection of mother and child. There are separate talks for men and women.

Middle-aged women are the hardest to persuade. Young women who already have three or four children are more than ready to come and listen; their husbands take more convincing, of course, for they don't have the job of actually bearing children. First they are taught the withdrawal method, then they are told how the condom and coil work. Naturally, there is some resistance to the use of the coil, for the young women fear it will cause haemorrhages; superstitions don't help.[5]

Three hundred women in the district have agreed to be fitted with a coil, out of a total population of 95,000. Abortions

5. Observations made by the surgeon in charge.

are carried out, provided there is mutual consent by husband and wife. In the case of a wife who has already borne three children, her own consent is sufficient.

The provincial hospital in Hung Yen has a staff of twelve surgeons and forty medical auxiliaries. They perform chest and kidney operations and brain surgery. Research is carried on there, in co-ordination with the district hospital. The senior surgeons at the provincial hospital are paid seventy dongs a month. At the district hospital, the surgeon in charge receives fifty-five dongs, the medical auxiliaries forty-five, and the orderlies thirty-six. There are fifty doctors and 800 medical auxiliaries in the province, to deal with 670,000 inhabitants. In 1954, there was only one doctor and four orderlies; in 1962, three doctors and thirty medical auxiliaries. These figures show how great an effort is being made to train staff, and they also indicate the amount of decentralization which has taken place within the medical service.

Trading

State trading developed in the years 1958–60. A nationalized trading circuit spread rapidly and now covers the entire home market. Barter has increased to a remarkable extent. Distribution of the raw materials needed for production and consumption alike is largely dominated by the state-controlled sector. In 1966, the state had about an 80 per cent share in the national distribution of consumer goods.

The state buys surplus rice from the co-operatives (0.27 dongs per kilo), together with other food and industrial crops, and also livestock (pigs, for instance, fetching 1.45 dongs per kilo). At provincial level there is a foreign trade board, while every district has a purchasing office which keeps in close touch with the local Party Committee, Administrative Committee and Trading Committee. The foreign trade board hands down the decisions of the Ministry for External Trade.

As soon as the produce has been assembled, the purchasing offices get an audit board to check their invoices and then dispatch the goods straight to the port of Haiphong without stockpiling them in the province. When the goods reach the port, they are inspected and placed in storage by the various major concerns handling particular commodities.

The village trading committee is also known as the purchasing co-operative. It buys produce for export directly from the peasants. It also buys from the co-operative. As a rule, the co-operative sells jute, pigs and ducks. The peasants sell their eggs and fruit. The prices paid for export are the same as those paid for domestic consumption. These prices are determined after talks between the ministry and the co-operatives. There is a national index, allowing for regional variations. In towns, the prices are higher.

Along the wayside, and especially at crossroads, are stalls displaying basket-loads of merchandise: this is the free market. A good many peasants contribute to it.

On the free market, a kilo of rice fetches 2.20 dongs. And for most other items the free-market price is four or five times higher than the state-controlled price.

Here are a few specimen prices charged by traders:

Kilo of small pond-fish: 2 dongs

10 top-grade bananas: 1 dong (0.50 dongs if second-grade)

1 egg: 0.45 dongs

7 oz. loaf: 0.40 dongs (state-fixed price 0.10 dongs)

Small orange: 0.25 dongs

Unripe lemon: 0.05 dongs

Box of matches: 0.15 dongs

1 rice-shape (0.50 g.): 0.50 dongs

1 biscuit: 0.10 dongs

1 cake (0.50 g.): 0.50 dongs

1 glass tea: 0.05 dongs

Small tangerine: 0.05 dongs

Litre of rice-fermented liquor: 7 dongs

If a peasant sells a live pig to the co-operative, he is paid 1.45 dongs per kilo; on the free market he can sell it for about five dongs per kilo. But he is only allowed to sell on the free market if he has already sold 75 to 80 per cent of his produce to the state. Anyone trading in the private sector must be officially registered and hold a licence. Each household keeps a careful record of everything which it has bought from, or sold to, the state. Special booklets have recently been issued for this purpose, and they can be proudly displayed as evidence of the contribution the family is making to the fight against aggression.

A few examples of earnings:

Schoolteacher (elementary)	35 dongs
Schoolteacher (higher grade)	41 dongs
Doctor	45–50 dongs
Surgeon	60–70 dongs
Highest earnings obtainable	250 dongs
Average annual monetary assets of a family of seven living in the delta region	100–600 dongs

Nguyen Quy's Accounts Book (Family of three)

The entries are recorded in a twenty-eight-page booklet, each page bearing the stamp and seal of the local Trading Committee. The booklet, signed by the Committee's representative, was issued in June 1967.

Table 14. Purchases

Date	Nature of goods	Amount	Price (in dongs)
12 June 67	Soap	1 (500g.)	0.67
	Matches	3	0.30
	Tea	1	0.30
			1.27
23 June 67	Oil	2 litres	2.50
26 July 67	Salted crayfish	2 litres	2.80
14 August 67	Sesame cake	1 (500g.)	} 1.35
	Reel of thread, needle and towel		
	Rice-fermented liquor	20 cl	0.20
10 October 67	Aluminium bowl	1	12.15

Table 15. Sales (to state, 1967).

Pig	1st	64 kilos	at 1.55 dongs per kilo
	2nd	64 kilos	

Any peasant selling pigs is entitled to buy back 30 per cent of the meat he has sold. If the animal he sells yields fifty kilos of treated meat, for example, he can repurchase seventeen kilos. He is not allowed to slaughter his own livestock. The state provides him with stamps entitling him to purchase at the following prices:

Leg	2.70 dongs per kilo
Shoulder	2.60 dongs per kilo
Belly	2.20 dongs per kilo
Loins	1.45 dongs per kilo
Head (with brain)	1.45 dongs per kilo

There is a black market, but not a very big one. It deals chiefly in oil, petrol, tobacco, sugar and pork. A kilo of pork fetches from seven to nine dongs on the black market; in Hanoi it fetches over ten dongs (official rate: 2.70 dongs). The state combats this traffic by releasing considerable quantities of goods at lower prices. Matches, for instance, were fetching 0.30 dongs a box on the black market in 1966. This price was forced down to 0.15 dongs when the state suddenly made a large supply of matches available.

The official price for a packet of cigarettes is 0.55 dongs, the black market price 1 dong.

Some items – e.g. petrol, sugar, tobacco – are unobtainable on the free market and can only be bought on the black market.

Official prices have fluctuated very little since escalation. Prices on the free market have increased by about 25 per cent. Rice was a dong per kilo in 1964; it rose to two dongs in 1965 and three dongs in 1966. To stabilize prices, the state had to sell rice at less than cost – the aim being to stimulate production and check the upward trend. Thanks to the increase in production in 1966–7, the price of rice on the free market was down to 1.80 dongs by the end of 1967. Prices are controlled by panels of experts operating at village level.

There is little or no custom at a village inn charging 1.50 dongs for a meal consisting of bread, three bananas, a rice-shape and a glass of tea. (A meal at a state canteen costs 0.50

dongs.) On the other hand, there is a regular breakfast-time queue outside a state-owned shop. The service is fairly quick, and for a hundred-gramme rice-coupon and 0.40 dongs, one can obtain a wheat cake (0.75 g.) and a cake containing sweet beans (160 g.). Supplies are soon exhausted, however, and the shop closes before the morning is over.

The free market makes up for the deficiencies of the state market, whose aim is (a) to supply the basic necessities at low prices and (b) to provide a guaranteed outlet for production.

Personal Statements

Phan Van Chu, peasant, aged sixty-one. Lives in a solid, well-furnished house in the village of Xich Dang (Kim Dong province). A huge portrait of Stalin hangs on one wall, and there are other, smaller portraits of Ho Chi Minh, General Giap and Mao Tse-tung:

I was born in this village, of a family of landless peasants. My father was from another village: he came here in search of work. One of the local peasants more or less adopted him, and he married the peasant's daughter. My father fished on the Red River, and my mother sold what he caught. My maternal grandfather had a sao of common land. I was the elder of two boys, and we had a little sister. There were no great landowners hereabouts – just rich peasants. So I went and worked for some of these rich peasants, minding buffaloes. I'm still illiterate, and because I'm old and my eyes are bad I've given up learning to read, although the Party urges us to make the effort. I've lived through three generations, and I'll do my best to think back and tell you what it was like.

Under the feudal regime there were lots of taxes, and we and most other villagers were denied an education. There was one school in our canton, but we stood no chance of going there: it was only for wealthy men's children. When we were old enough to start paying taxes – eighteen – we were given a plot of land to work, down by the river. But as the taxes were very high, a man was unable to hold on to his land and had to sell it to the rich. Sometimes he had no sooner been given a plot than he had to sell it so as to pay the debts. I had a plot measuring eight saos, and I kept it for three years, and then I had to cede it to a peasant for thirty piastres because of a three-year loan he had made me. Unless I repaid him within three years, I had to sell the land to him. I was lucky: the effort nearly wore me out, but at the end of the three years I managed to get my land back. After five years' work, I had to part with the land again – surrendering a three-year lease for about thirty piastres. But I made sure my plot was restored to me when the three years were up, and I held on to it until the Revolution.

In the old days, we had to do forced labour when we were eighteen. Among other things, we were obliged to put up buildings for the Residents, the mandarins and the French. We had to garden for them, too. Sometimes, mandarins would leave the province and move to Thai Binh. The villagers had to trudge along behind, carrying their belongings. This meant a trek of thirty or forty miles, with no rest at night; they gave us very little to eat, and they didn't pay us for the work. The provincial administrators were French, and the heads of cantons were Vietnamese. We didn't have any contact with the mandarins. We didn't have any contact with the French, either, for we couldn't speak their language and didn't know much about them. But the French customs officers used to come searching for liquor, and sometimes they caught unlicensed vendors and operators of illicit stills. They confiscated the liquor and jailed those who had been handling it. Anyone who couldn't afford to hire lawyers and grease the right palms might spend three, four or even five years in prison. My own family were too poor to do any trafficking, but some of the other villagers got caught and sent to jail.

We had four property-owners here in the village. During the land reform programme, they were seized and packed off to internment camps. There they spent four, five and in one case eight years. Now they have all returned and are members of the co-operative. There was never any doubt about their guilt: they had all been landowners and elders. In our village, the land reform programme was carried out without mistakes of any kind: not a single Party member was attacked.

After the first nineteen households had joined the co-operative, our family joined too; it must have been late in 1960 or early in 61. I contributed an ox at a price fixed by the co-operative. What made us join? Patriotism and enthusiasm, that's all. The spread of irrigation staved off drought, and we gradually increased the yield. By 1963 there was a distinct improvement, and we had 700 extra kilos of rice. In 1966 our family made

4,500 points, while livestock, fish, manure and so on earned us nearly 350 dongs. We have three mouths to feed, and two full-time workers. Life is certainly better than it was. Electricity has come to the village. But now, because of the fighting, we must speed up production; many of our number have gone off to join the army, and we need to send supplies to the South. We have managed to stabilize prices and contribute more to the state-controlled market. We believe that President Ho will lead us to victory, and that the nation will one day be reunited.

Vu Huy Hoc, peasant, aged fifty-one, born 'right here in the village of Xich Dang', in the district of Kim Dong. He lives in modern, stone-built house with a thatched roof. Inside, four diplomas are on display: the Resistance Medal; a certificate congratulating him for good work; a certificate testifying to his active contribution as a member of the land army; a certificate to show that he belongs to the security service. The furniture consists of a chest, a table, two benches, a hammock, two double beds with mosquito netting, and a loudspeaker. On the far side of the threshing-floor is a brick-built outside kitchen measuring seven feet by seven. No cistern, but a septic tank. In 1966 he achieved 4,000 points. He has a family of five, including two full-time and two part-time workers. His allotment covers an area of one sao. His pigs, poultry and vegetables earned him about 540 dongs in 1966. In addition, he sold 500 kilos of rice, ten tons of manure and a Mercier bicycle. (The latter fetched 700 dongs on the free market, the purchaser being a member of the co-operative who needed the cycle for carrying goods.) This made a grand total of about 1,500 dongs – i.e. half the 3,000 dongs it cost him to build the house he lives in today:

My family owned five saos, but in addition they hired themselves out to landowners. I had one brother and one sister. My brother is dead, but my sister lives here in the village. We didn't receive any education until after the Revolution, but since then I've completed two classes. I was hired out to a rich peasant, too; I ploughed for him.

I did my bit in the first war of resistance. There was a school for NCOs in this area – nearly 300 of them, manning five posts. In 1951 or 52 the Vietminh guerrillas started harassing them, and they gradually withdrew.

Under the land reform programme, our family got eight saos. There were four of us at the time. I earned a good living in the days of private ownership. I had nearly twelve hundred-weight of rice; I also had maize, pigs (first one, then two) and a dozen birds, not to mention fruit and vegetables. I was making nearly 300 piastres. All the same, I was one of the first to join the co-operative, for what I had been told made me feel I would be better off if I did. Collectivization brought me many advantages: for instance, there are now three harvests a year, a rice harvest, a jute harvest and a maize harvest; you can earn a lot if you work hard. I've been able to send my son and daughter to school. Today my son is in the army, and my daughter is in Class 8 at the provincial school. I'm free to go on with my studies, too – I am now at Class 3 standard. We no longer have any real worries about the future. There is never any shortage of reserves when Tet draws near. And another thing: we are free to put up our own candidates for the People's Council.

But we have the American aggression to contend with, of course. The Americans are grabbing Vietnam's resources in the South and destroying everything we have built in the North. They're doing it because they want to be masters of the world. They must be driven out at all costs. On our side, the aggression is compelling us to step up production – for that is essential if we are to feed the army and help our brothers in the South. In this area, we shall soon have reached two tons an acre; we might even manage it this year. Previously there were doubts about internal unity. But now we simply must be united if we are to produce more and achieve victory; and, thanks to this unity, we are getting good results and making progress. I should love to become a Party member, but I'm not up to the required standards yet, so I'm just an ordinary co-operator. It's hard to explain exactly what these standards are. You have to achieve good production figures; you have to play an active part in all that is going on; you have to do a lot for the community. The Party workers are the cream of the village, the torch-bearers – I don't belong among them yet.

Doan Van Hoc, peasant, aged forty-five, foreman of a team of seven fruit-tree planters. He owns a solid stone house furnished with a bed, a table, two armchairs, two benches and a chest:

My parents used to peddle rice. They owned two and a half saos, but that wasn't enough to keep them going so they took to trade. My father did the husking and my mother did the selling. They were both natives of this village: it used to be called Trieu Duong and had something like 2,000 inhabitants in those days. I was born here, just like my parents. We were poor, and I had to help my parents with the jobs. I received an elementary education. I was the eldest of three children, two boys and one girl. We were very poor just then, so I couldn't stay on at school. I used to help my mother sell the rice and go out and catch crabs for us to eat. I started school at nine or ten and remained there for four years. As I say, we had only two and a half saos of land; but we managed to build a cottage bit by bit. The house we're living in now wasn't built till 1965. My mother died when I was twenty-five, and my father followed her three years later.

In those days, there used to be special ceremonies to commemorate ancestors. For these, you had to haul in some fish and kill a chicken, if you *had* a chicken; otherwise you went out and caught a few crabs. On ordinary days, we only ate one meal: rice soup with bran.

My younger brother didn't get much education, and my sister only went to nursery school. There was a landowner called Tinh, who was the wealthiest of the dozen landowners in the village. This landowner decided to put up a two-storey house, complete with outbuildings and a threshing-floor, and my father helped to erect it. This was in 1945, at a time of great famine, and my father worked without pay, just to get his hands on something to eat. The house took three months to finish, and that was what kept us alive – for, although my father didn't get much food, he used to bring some home. Our family was in debt: we borrowed from this landowner at an interest rate of 10 per cent per month. From time to time we also borrowed rice at an interest rate of 50 per cent, to be repaid after the next harvest. Being in trade, we borrowed more money than rice. On one occasion my father had to give up two saos of his land, which left us with only half a sao; and since we had no money to repay the debt, we were compelled to leave the two saos in the hands of the landowner. This man Tinh was in the Council of Notables; he was known as Ba Ho, a nickname implying that he was wealthy enough to own a hundred homes. [*Ba* means a hundred, *Ho* means home.]

It didn't happen to my family, but some peasants were tortured when the tax collectors came round. We always managed to raise a small amount, but people who couldn't afford to pay were bound and tortured. In those days the village formed part of a canton, which had an official chief. If a landowner was short-handed, he could send his agents out to recruit labour. The unemployed used to take their hats and gourds and wait in the courtyard of the pagoda, hoping that the landowner's agents would come and hire them. If no agent came, they would leave the district and look for work elsewhere.

At New Year, or on the fifth day of the fifth lunar month, it was the custom to hold a feast at the communal house. Everyone was seated according to rank. Animals were slaughtered and eaten in honour of the spirits.

I married a local girl when I was twenty; she was twenty-two. I had to take a pig's head to her father's house, together with betel nuts, betel leaves, rice liquor and a plucked chicken. [*At this point his wife, who was sitting beside us, laughed.*] A year later, we had our first child; we've had six in all, and three have survived. The others died at a very early age, because of the unhygienic conditions and the general lack of medicine.

If you wanted to go to another village, you had to have a pass bearing the seal of Ly Truong (the mayor) – otherwise you were arrested. My own family came through the great famine unscathed, but there were over a hundred deaths in the village. Those who managed to get jobs on the landowners' estates were all right, but many of the unemployed starved to death. At that point the Revolution started, and the Vietminh arrived in the district to take over the stocks of rice which the Japanese had built up. They seized the rice and shared it out among the neediest: bereaved families were the first to benefit. The People's Committee put out appeals, urging people to join up: some of the younger villagers were quite ready to enlist; but others were afraid to, for they were none too clear what all this might lead to; they weren't sure what 'liberating the country' really meant. The war between the French and the Japanese had given place to a war between the Vietminh and the French. My younger brother volunteered for service, and today he is a captain.

I didn't really know what the Vietminh was. Also, I was scared: I was chary of joining them because I couldn't see what good they would do us. But we weren't afraid of them, for they weren't out to harm us.

By 1947 I had seen the light, and I did my bit by becoming a village security agent, checking people's papers, tracking down poultry thieves, that kind of thing. I wasn't treated to a lot of propaganda: I just noticed how different they were from the Japanese, who used to grab our rice or else make us pull it up and plant jute instead. We gradually came to realize that our army had our interests at heart. Also, I heard of the victories which our troops had won in this province and others besides.

Late in 1949, or early in 1950, the French army – the whites – came to Trieu Duong dam, less than a mile from here, and started building a post for about a hundred men; they far outnumbered the platoon of Moroccans at the post at Haiyen, only 500 yards away. The French formed the landowners into a Council of Notables. Then they called all the rest of us together and made us carry bamboo and bricks for them. I had to go to the Pagoda, two miles from here, remove the bricks from the building – with the Moroccans standing over me – and deliver them to the post. Once they beat me so hard that my thighs were badly swollen, just because they thought I wasn't moving fast enough. Trieu Duong was a flooded area, so an embankment had to be built; but hardly any peasants turned up, and the French assumed that the Vietminh had told us not to do any more forced labour. Their answer was to shell the village. More than fifty people were killed. Apart from the French forces, there were about a hundred puppet troops. Sometimes they would disguise themselves as peasants, come into the village and ambush the Vietminh. They would break into the landowner's house, get drunk, take a bath in his reservoir, and then make off with some of our poultry. Sometimes they would set a time limit for the elders to supply them with poultry and pigs, and if this time limit wasn't met they would shell the village. That happened twice. People got killed and several houses were completely destroyed. In 1946 and 47, the guerrilla movement was very weak: there were five or six of them in the village; they would fire a few shots and then bolt as soon as the whites or the Moroccans or the puppet troops appeared. As a reprisal, the enemy would set fire to houses, take hostages, and demand money and food from the elders. People who had been slow to back the Vietminh were likewise subjected to acts of terrorism, and so they began to support the guerrillas, and some joined forces with them. In 1952, regular Vietminh forces brought up artillery and started shelling the posts, and the guerrillas helped them as much as they could by passing on information and carrying out diversionary and delaying tactics. During the enemy's mopping-up operations, a lot of women got raped – especially by the Moroccans. There were at least fifty victims right here in the village. Afterwards, we had to take them to the first-aid post for attention: they were in a bad way. The French raped five or six of the girls doing forced labour at their post in Trieu Duong.

I used to go and buy rice from other areas, for – quite apart from the damage caused by shelling – we didn't have enough to go round. Buying and selling kept me alive. Two things happened round about 1954: the B26s destroyed half the village, and we liquidated the Council of Elders.

With independence came land reform. I had a fifth of a sao. I was given another fifth to build a house on, and two saos for growing rice. My wife and I had to turn the new land over with spades and forks, for we had no buffalo to pull the plough. It made us so happy to own a plot of land for the first time in our lives. Sometimes we even worked at night, and we reaped good harvests. I worked really hard on my land for four years, and we reaped good harvests every year. Early in 1956 I began to build a new house, converting the old cottage into a kitchen. I gradually scraped the building materials together. Then I started laying the foundations, without anyone to help me, in the hope of finishing the job by the end of the year. Twenty-two thousand bricks were needed in all, and I bought them as I went along, a few hundred at a time, stacking them till I had enough. Eventually I got a bricklayer to help me. He came at the beginning of 1957 and we finished the house together. I didn't have any roof-timber; we just built the walls, and we didn't finish those until the end of 1957, working as and when we were able and as and when I could afford bricks. Up to that point I had spent 1,500 dongs out of my own pocket, and I had to go to relations and borrow another 2,000 – free of interest. I bought the timber from a house belonging to a man who had been wrongly classified as a landowner; when the mistakes of the land reform programme were put right, he was reclassified as a rich peasant; so he was entitled to sell part of his property. This 'landowner' had three small houses. The one he sold me had been hit by shellfire, and I only bought it for the sake of the roof-timber, which was still in good condition.

At the end of the four years I mentioned earlier, I was able to pay back all I had borrowed. As we were only reaping one harvest a year, I continued to buy and sell; and all in all I earned quite a comfortable living. I went to Hanoi to buy a cupboard: it cost me 200 dongs and I brought it here by boat. This bed was made in 1965; before that, all I had was a bamboo trestle and a mat. Since 1965 I have also managed to get a mosquito net, which cost thirty dongs. I paid thirty dongs for the table and benches. The two joss-sticks were left to me by my father; so was the flower vase, which I use when I am commemorating his anniversary.

By 1958 people were beginning to join the co-operative, but I wasn't keen. I wanted to be free to sell my rice, for I was doing well out of it. At that stage there were only twenty-eight families in the co-operative. Early in 1960 I changed my mind and joined. I'll tell you why: it was getting harder to sell my rice, for controls had been brought in, and I was having to operate on the black market. Previously, I had made more out of buying and selling other people's rice than out of growing my own. When converted into paddy, my earnings as a dealer were sufficient to feed us throughout the year – and there were usually a couple of hundredweights left over. On the other hand, the rice we grew at home was only enough to cover sundry expenses like family ceremonies and a few new bits and pieces. After the controls were introduced, I began to smuggle the rice to market, displaying only a portion of my wares in one basket. My other basket was full of rice, but I covered it over with banana leaves. This extra rice escaped detection, and so I managed to sell more than I was officially allowed to. I kept it up for two years, until 1960.

I had my own fruit trees, and a small pond for breeding fish, and I felt there was no point in becoming a member of the co-operative. But officials came to see me and said: 'Join, and you will enjoy a better standard of living. You may be comfortably off now, but you'll do even better in the co-operative.' They kept on and on about it, and in the end I joined, thinking it would benefit me. There was a good harvest in the summer of 1960, but the returns were poorer than those I'd had in previous years. So I asked permission to leave the co-operative. The officials in charge didn't like this at all. Yes, they said, the harvest was a good one, but not as good as it ought to have been, for the rice had yellowed; our co-operative would do better in future; when times were bad I would enjoy the benefits of mutual aid, and at the Lunar New Year I would receive my share of fish from the co-operative. 'In this way,' I was told, 'you are helping to make the country stronger. You must be patriotic.'

But I saw how my earnings had fallen off, and I thought: 'I don't need a share of their fish. I've a pond of my own, and with the fish I breed I can buy more rice – to say nothing of the rice we grow on our own land.'

I realized that everyone was joining the co-operative in an

effort to build a strong nation, and I could see this was a patriotic thing to do. But it was the idea of collective ownership that bothered me; for private land yielded sufficient, whereas co-operative land yielded less. So I kept on pressing them for permission to leave, and after a few months they said: 'Very well – you may leave, since you are so keen to.' But I only missed one harvest. Early in 1961 I asked to be readmitted, for the following reasons. My trading activities kept me so busy that I had to pay other people to work my land and catch fish from my pond; but all these people were now working in the co-operative, with the result that labour had become more expensive and they were no longer willing to work at the old rates of pay. This meant I didn't make enough profit. Besides, all the time I was out of the co-operative I didn't get any meat coupons, for they were only distributed to co-operators. I asked my relations what they thought I should do, and applied for readmission. Returns had been good that year. There had been two harvests, thanks to the new dikes.

At first I was turned down and told: 'It was all thoroughly explained to you, and yet you left.' But I didn't give up, and after a fortnight they accepted me. 'There must be no more quibbling, though,' they said. 'We told you before: the idea is to achieve a higher standard of living by pooling our resources. But you wouldn't believe us; you preferred to listen to outsiders who ran us down.' I had to give a written undertaking not to listen to any more lying slanders against the co-operative: this time I must join for good and work on the land like everyone else; if I left a second time, I would forfeit the right to my two saos and my pond. I signed this agreement and handed it in. I gave up buying and selling, and my wife and I worked on the land. We earned a lot of points. In the first harvest of 1961 we acquired enough rice for the family to live on, and in addition I was able to sell two hundredweights to the state. In the second harvest I sold three hundredweights to the state, at the rate of 2.70 dongs per ten kilos. Also, I got sixty dongs for my share of the co-operative's fish.

In 1962 the returns were adequate, though there was a smaller surplus than in previous years – a hundredweight of rice from the first harvest and four hundredweights from the second, plus fifty dongs for the fish. But I managed to acquire items which other co-operatives were allowed to sell at state-controlled prices (which are far lower than the prices on the free market): sugar, beans, tobacco, clothing materials and oil. We built a large defensive dike around our village, and we've been able to reap two harvests a year ever since. I didn't do much towards building the dike, for I suffer from elephantiasis and am not allowed to wade about in the water; but I made up for this by helping with tasks on dry land.

Nowadays I work in the fruit-tree plantation, while my wife works in the fields. I plant longans and orange trees. There are sixty people in my working party, including twenty old men and thirty old women; the rest are children between the ages of ten and fifteen. The work is shared out so that the weakest do the light jobs, while the strongest do the digging. Work begins at seven and goes on till eleven, with a short break at nine. One of us does the watering, another does the weeding, and a third plants new shrubs. In the afternoons we work from two till five, picking fruit and so on. I'm given rice in the fifth lunar month, and again in the tenth. Since 1962 I've been able to afford a cycle (275 dongs), a pair of blankets (100 dongs), two flower vases (sixty dongs), and a mosquito net (twenty-five dongs). I'm contented, and I love living in this village. My family has lived here for generations: in accordance with ancient custom, my umbilical cord was cut off and buried in local soil, and my father's body is buried here too. How can anyone leave his native village without regrets? We live surrounded by our kith and kin, and we can always turn to relations when times are bad. And there is plenty of helpful give and take between ourselves and the neighbours: we grew up with them, and in the old days we shared food when it was short, and we have borne heavy burdens together. There is nothing to stop us from earning our living elsewhere, but it wouldn't be the same.

The important thing now is that we should produce more, so as to drive the Americans out; then we shall be able to live in peace and work our land without being bombed. We *are* producing more, to feed the army that is safeguarding our lives and labours and defending our country. The Americans are destroying everything we have worked so hard to build; they must get out of our country – and that includes the South. When peace comes, I shall be able to give my children more; most important of all, they will no longer have to live in dugouts. Why should men of other countries live above ground, when we have to live below it?

Hoang Van Sun, peasant, aged forty-two, living in the village of Hoang Ca. According to his points book, he and his wife and their seventeen-year-old son earned a total of 8,000 points in 1966. The son made nearly 1,000, and the parents 7,000. They own a soundly built modern house with two ground-floor rooms, a concrete drying-floor, a septic tank, a cistern, and half a sao of land for growing vegetables. They have five children. The eldest boy has completed ten full years at school and is now at the university. A daughter, aged fifteen, goes to school and minds the buffalo. A twelve-year-old boy goes to school and tends the geese, while another boy, aged nine, attends lessons in the morning and does jobs in the afternoon. In 1966, this peasant sold 250 dongs-worth of rice to the state (i.e. about sixteen hundredweights). He also sold two hundredweights on the free market, for 200 dongs. His allotment earned him fifty dongs, and his livestock and poultry 680 dongs (he received 280 from the sale of pigs, and 400 from the sale of geese); but some of this had to be deducted for feeding costs, leaving 250 dongs. Altogether, he calculates, he earned forty-two hundredweights of rice and about 1,170 dongs in 1966. He is a 'rich peasant':

My father was a gambler, a rake and a heavy drinker. From 1938 until 1943 he worked at a Tonkinese coal mine in Cam Pha (Haiphong). My mother spent those years toiling as a pedlar in Hanoi, though sometimes she took jobs on building sites, carrying bricks in the buckets of her yoke. I lived with her in Hanoi until I was twenty. My parents didn't own any land then – they weren't peasants any longer. But I was born in the village and lived here with my parents until I was thirteen. We had only half a sao of land; my father lost so heavily at cards that he was forced to sell it, and we had to move to the city. I had learned to read and write by then. The village schoolmaster (this was in 1935 or 36) was a scholar who taught Vietnamese. My father gambled away the wages he earned at the mine, leaving my mother to feed and clothe the whole family. I was one of six children. Two married very early, so she had four of us to bring up in Hanoi. We lived in a cottage near the bridge over the Red River. My mother sold sawdust and firewood, and I sold newspapers: *Dong Phap* ['France Oriental'] and *Phoi Moi* ['New Times']. My married sisters had stayed behind in the village. My brothers and sisters used to help my mother sell vegetables at the market; she did this every day, on top of all her other work. These various jobs earned us enough to live on, and we gave up going to school.

In 1944 my father joined us in Hanoi and started hawking goods to the Japanese. He delivered merchandise from the airport to the shops. He was killed during an Allied raid on the airport in 1945. When the Japanese took over, we moved back to the village. We stayed with my aunt. I brewed liquor, which was against the law. We bred ducks, for the sake of the eggs, and my mother – who was getting on by that time – stayed at home and fed the pigs. We built an extension to my aunt's house and lived there for a year and a half. Then I built a bamboo house, so that we could live by ourselves. We were short of food during the famine, but no one in the family died. In the first war of resistance I joined the local self-defence group and also the peasants' association. One day in 1948 or 49 they raided and searched the village and burnt nearly all the houses; I managed to slip away. I also helped with the farming. We had half a sao. We worked hard, and I bought the land which had been sold. Altogether, using the money we earned by breeding pigs and ducks, we bought a mau of rice-growing land.

Then came the land reform programme. We had a good many mouths to feed, so we were given another eight saos. Sometimes we reaped two harvests a year. This enabled us to save, and we produced good results. In those days I used to sell on the free market, and I earned a lot of money. We sold a ton and a half of rice a year at two or three hundred piastres a ton. In 1961 I joined the co-operative. Everyone else had joined, so I joined too. I didn't join straightaway – not until after the first two harvests. I joined in answer to the Party's appeal. I didn't belong to the Party at the time, though I have now been a member for the past four years. At first I got less out of working for the co-operative than in the days when I had been working independently. We only saved six hundred-weights of rice, and of course I couldn't help noticing the difference. The co-operative has come a long way since then. The standard of living has risen, as a result of technical improvements, the scientific use of fertilizers, and recent developments in irrigation. It is now common practice for us to reap two, and sometimes three, harvests a year, whereas most people only reaped one in the old days. When I joined the co-operative, I contributed my paddy-field and a third of a bullock (three of us had clubbed together to buy the animal). I had three saos of pondwater and my own farming tools.

Since the attacks started, we have dug trenches and organized an anti-aircraft defence system. We have responded to the Party's appeals and are doing our best to ensure our safety, for where there is human life there is the possibility of producing things of value. Today we are trying to grow more of everything, so that we may keep the army fed and win the war. Early in the year, bombs were dropped on paddy-fields less than two miles away. One woman was killed and several people wounded. Also, several houses have been destroyed in night raids.

Do Thi Vien, aged twenty-one, member of the commune's Administrative Committee, spinster:

I was born here in the village, one of four girls. The other three are all married and have children. I still live with my parents. My father is seventy, my mother sixty-five. My father earns points by looking after the oxen, and my mother runs the house. In the old days my father owned five saos; today he has only the ground we live on. We were 'poor peasants'.

I first went to school when I was eleven; before that, I used to help my mother about the house and look after the buffaloes. I began my education late because we were poor. My sisters took outside jobs and received only three years' schooling. I don't remember much about the first war of resistance, but I recall how my family had to move to another village and work for landowners. Then, in 1954, we came back to our own village and were given a plot of land under the land reform programme. I used to study in the mornings and lend a hand with the work in the afternoons. From Class 1 to Class 4, I attended a school near home; but from Class 5 to Class 7 I had to travel a mile and a half each way and afterwards help the family in the fields. When my schooldays were over, I sat an examination to get into the post office. That was in 1963, at a time when the government was urging people to return to their native villages and improve the standards of farming. I did as they suggested.

At first I regretted breaking off my education, for I wanted to become a party official. But once I started working here, I was glad to be in the countryside.

Apart from lessons, we did singing and dancing and PT and games at school. We also had an area of land for experimental work, and we spent half a day each week helping in the fields and with the fish-breeding. We dug new ponds, and occasionally we did a bit of dam-building or irrigating. I really loved school-work. I'd have liked to do historical research. I'm very busy these days, but I still find time to read textbooks and documents. Now that the Party has chosen me for this work, I find it interesting; I want to go on with it and do better at it.

I help to look after the commune's financial affairs. I also deal with births, deaths and marriages, making a monthly return to the district authorities. The state leaves the commune to manage its own properties – the fish-ponds, for instance, and the fruit trees along the roads. The Committee deducts a share of the proceeds and pays it into the commune's account; it is part of my job to record these takings.

As a rule, the commune keeps 10 per cent of the sums raised by the sale of fish and fruit. The remainder is passed on to the co-operators. If there are natural disasters, I make an on-the-spot study of the problem and send a report to the district and provincial authorities, and we lower the percentage deducted by the commune.

It is also my job to supervise buying and selling. I have to make sure that financial affairs are being properly managed and that stocks are not running too high. In addition, I have to keep an eye on loans from the state. For instance, it is up to me to ensure that the best possible use is made of the money which a co-operative may have borrowed to install a pumping station. The aim is to keep waste to a minimum.

The commune invests its savings in the district or provincial authorities, keeping careful records of the sums deposited and the interest due; that is another of my responsibilities. Again, whenever consignments of goods arrive it is my job to check them in and see that they are fairly distributed; otherwise they might find their way on to the black market, or the officials might slip them to their own families. I examine the household records of sales and purchases, to make sure that the item in question has not been bought before – for it is important that goods should go to those who really need them. Abuses are rare, but they do occur. For example, we caught one retailer selling mats 'under the counter'. He was hauled before the district supervisory board and given a lecture on the Party's trading policies. Anyone guilty of this kind of thing has to appear before the assembled members of the commune and make public acknowledgement of the offence. His goods are impounded, if he still has any; but he is reimbursed at the official rate and allowed to go free. Nobody in these parts has committed the same offence twice.

Since early 1966 I've been a member of the militia, like most young people here. I've taken a four-week course in handling a machine-gun. In the old days, under the feudal regime, women stood no chance of achieving equal opportunities with men. Today all that has changed: we can play a full part in every sphere of activity. I've been a Party member since July 1966; more and more of us are joining the Party, especially young people. Our main problem at present is how to produce more and at the same time resist aggression. We are determined to fight, in North and South alike, and we are sure of victory.

The Americans may have tremendous military strength, but they are weaker than us in terms of international political support.

Doan Thi Thanh, peasant, aged nineteen, unmarried. She lives in a stone house with an outside kitchen and a water tank. There is only one room, containing a double bed (with a mosquito net), a hammock, a cot, a table, two benches and a cupboard. On the walls are portraits of Ho Chi Minh, Mao Tse-tung, Lenin and Pham Van Dong:

I was born in the village in 1948, at the height of the revolution. I live here in this house, which was built in 1957, with my mother, my brother's wife and her little girl. I am a member of the local youth movement, and I also belong to the women's militia. There are twenty-one girls in the platoon, and we have been trained for active service. Another group of women – wives and mothers, a dozen in all – perform other duties for the militia, mainly transport and supply work.

Before 1954, we had three fifths of a sao. We had no paddy-fields of our own, so my mother bought and sold other people's rice. Between them, she and my father earned enough to send me and my brother to school. My brother had been educated up to Class 10 standard by the time he joined the army – he is still in the service. My father was a schoolmaster; from 1945 to 1950 he was in the district security branch of the Vietminh. From 1950 to 1961 he worked for the provincial authorities, as an official in the finance department. My mother was here in the village all that time, working on the land. When I was in Class 9 my father died, and I had to come home and help my mother. Since 1959, my mother has not been strong enough to work. She stays at home and looks after the house, while my sister-in-law and I supply the full-time labour.

My family was one of the first to join the co-operative in 1959. We benefited from the change: after my father died, we received extra rice to make up for the money he used to send us. And slowly but surely life has become more comfortable. For the past three years I have been working with my sister-in-

law and applying the technical knowledge I acquired at school:
I already knew a lot about cross-breeding, seed selection, the
use of fertilizers, the importance of planting rice in a straight
line, and so on. I was then in a 'mixed' group of men and girls.
Within the group was a team of six technicians, four girls
(including myself) and two men. The skills I had learned at
school enabled me to earn almost as many points as a top-grade
worker.

Until 1963 the co-operative had no proper control over
water-levels. We were subject to flooding and drought. We
used to lose a lot of fish, for the water overflowed the dikes.
Sometimes our rice got flooded, too. Things like that don't
happen any more. Today I'm a technician in a rice-production
group. I deal with such matters as pricking out, selection of
fertilizers, duckweed and water control. Ours is a low-lying
area, and fields containing young rice plants used to be drained
in the old days – for a heavy downfall might well produce eight
inches of rain. This draining was harmful to the rice, which
always needs water. Now we have sound dikes and are able to
keep the water at a constant level of four inches.

I am out in the fields with the others by 6.30 a.m.; there
are eighty of us in the working party. We work till eleven. Each
technician is attached to a particular group, in charge of pricking
out, spreading manure, and so forth. We start again after the
midday meal and stop at 5 p.m. For lunch we have rice, bind-
weed and soused shrimps. We get fish two or three times a
week, and meat two or three times a month. The evening meal
is lighter, with less rice: we have maize and sweet potato, with
soup at times and occasionally fruit. I'm allowed just over
three yards of clothing material a year. I have one dress for
work and one for wearing about the house.

Each working party meets twice a month, to discuss production problems. Other groups hold meetings, too – the youth
club, for instance, and the militia. In addition, young people of
both sexes have a weekly get-together, at which they sing
songs and put on plays. Those of us who are in the militia go
on the firing range once a week; we are also taught how to lay
mines and throw grenades. Naturally, we still find time for

relaxation; we like to read the life-stories of heroes and heroines like Nguyen Van Troi, Nguyen Viet Xuan and Hoang Ngan.

What difference has the American aggression made to my life and the life of the co-operative as a whole?

Since the raids started, we have been making every effort to produce more. In normal times, we used to produce just over a ton and a half per acre; now we produce two. We do more work. Many of the men have joined the army, and yet we've dug trenches everywhere and we've trained really hard and we're ready to deal with air attacks at a moment's notice. There was a raid two miles from here at the beginning of the year: seventy people were killed, but we shot down one of the planes. With so many of the men away on active service, we women have taken on posts of ever-increasing responsibility. We are held in higher esteem today, for we have achieved good results – better, in some cases, than the men themselves achieved. Of course, menstruation tends to stand in the way of equality, and so does pregnancy; but they make no basic difference. Some of the jobs in the fields – ploughing and harrowing, for instance – used to be regarded as men's work; but we've managed to get over that. The old people say: 'In the old days, we had to depend on the men. Now the girls do everything the men used to do.'

Vu Ngoc Nuoi, peasant, aged sixty:

My grandfather had five sons and two daughters. Four of his sons starved to death in 1945, my father among them. My father worked as a hired labourer. He had no land of his own, nor had my mother. She's eighty-four and still with us. I had two brothers and two sisters, but they all died of disease long ago.

When I was fifteen, I used to go and catch fish from the ponds. At sixteen I became a labourer on an estate. Life was grim in those days. We lived in a small hut with a few pots and pans but no bed. We had to work from five in the morning till six at night, with a thirty-minute meal-break: the landowner used to give us some rice mixed with maize and a few pickled vegetables. We were paid next to nothing: two hundredths of a piastre for a day's work, when a kilo of rice cost a whole piastre. In times of famine, we were given food instead of money.

I used to practise ancestor worship, and I still do. We hold special ceremonies on the anniversaries of our parents' deaths, offering up a salver of rice and other foodstuffs and burning a few joss-sticks. Relations come to the house and join in. In the old days we held a ceremony on the tenth day of the second lunar month in honour of a spirit known as Quoc – I forget what he ever did for the village. And on the seventh day of the third lunar month there was another ceremony for a goddess called Mau – at least, I *think* that was her name. Every family had to contribute thirty sous for these two feasts, though it was the notables who wolfed all the food. If we failed to scrape the money together, they would have us locked up. We had to ask for time to pay, and they wrote down all the particulars, and we had to put our thumb-mark on the document. If we didn't pay up within the agreed period, we were arrested a second time and beaten until we raised the money. We didn't dare borrow from the landowners, for their interest rates were so high that there was no chance of ever paying them back. Now we celebrate the New Year and our national day (2 September).

On top of all this, we had to pay the capitation tax levied by the French. The charge was between 2 piastres and 2 piastres 50. There were green cards for the really poor, yellow cards for those who were slightly better off, and red cards for the wealthy. From time to time, French customs officers would come and search our homes for liquor, for we were not allowed to make it.

During the first war of resistance I was a member of the local militia, and we hid some of the ringleaders in our house. I took part in quite a few operations, serving as a stretcher-bearer or transporting supplies of rice and water. I had five children at the time, and we had to send them into the enemy-occupied zone; my wife travelled to and fro, while I stayed behind and got on with the work. We sent the children away on account of the continual raids and searches. I wanted them to live in safety and get on with their education, so I placed them in the care of some of our agents who were working under cover behind the enemy's lines. I was caught in one of the raids on the village – luckily I had managed to hide my gun. The raid was carried out by French commandos. They beat me up and took me to the post at Trieu Duong. There they gave me another beating-up and started torturing me. They tied a rag over my mouth and pumped water into me until my stomach nearly burst; then they put their weight on me, to make the water run out through my mouth. In the afternoon they gave me more of the same treatment. They kept on asking me about the ringleaders I had sheltered, and I said: 'I haven't done anything wrong, I'm just a peasant.' On the second day, the French interrogator strung me up by the thumbs, set me swinging to and fro, and beat me till I passed out. He had a Vietnamese interpreter with him. This went on for a whole week, from first thing in the morning till last thing at night. Afterwards they made me go with them on a mopping-up operation. I had to carry crates of ammunition for them. But they walked into an ambush, and I managed to get away during the fighting.

In those days we were very poor; we didn't get enough to eat; we were badly knocked about. We were glad when the uprising came, for it meant things were going to turn out just as the propaganda people had said. Shall I tell you why I didn't talk when they beat me? Because they were too arrogant towards us: they treated us as though we were cattle. Anyway, we really hated the enemy on account of the looting and the butchery we had seen with our own eyes. That is why I threw in my lot with the Vietminh. Things are very different today: we have quite a comfortable house, enough to eat, and a school for our children to go to. We owe all that to the Party.

In 1954 the government gave us a mau and a half of land. I promptly joined one of the mutual-aid groups. Later I became a co-operator, and our standard of living improved – for we had a surplus which we could sell to the state. Improving the yields called for hard work. We had to cut canals. We planted fruit trees during the hours of daylight and cut canals after dark.

Now we have taken up bee-keeping. The old people in the commune have been getting a pound of honey a year, and they will get more as the bee-keeping co-operative grows. We eat three meals a day, with fish two or three times a week and an occasional helping of meat.

We are a peace-loving people; but the enemy has attacked us, and so we have called up our sons and nephews and sent them to the front, while we stay here and produce as much as we can. The more damage they inflict on us, the more we hate them, and we are doing our best to produce extra so that we can hold out and win. I have two sons in the NLF. They've been fighting in the South for the past two years.

Both of them came home on a week's leave last May, but just missed seeing each other. They're twenty-four and twenty-two. They say the enemy isn't fighting as hard as he used to; they reckon things are going our way.

Vu Chi Thanh, peasant, aged thirty-one, living in the village of Hoang Ka (Hoang Thu commune). His thatch-roofed house contains four beds – including two camp-beds – an indoor brick-lined trench, a table, two benches, and a makeshift altar for ancestor worship:

My parents worked as labourers on a local estate. We once owned half a sao, but had to sell it to pay off debts; the buyer was another peasant, better off than ourselves, though he certainly wasn't a big landowner. I was the third of five children: I have two elder brothers and two sisters. I started school in 1947 and reached Class 4 standard. Both my brothers reached Class 2 standard; one of my sisters went as far as Class 6, the other as far as Class 3. By the time I was seven, I was helping my parents with various jobs like looking after the pigs and poultry. We couldn't afford a buffalo or a bullock. We used to buy rice straight from the fields, husk it, and sell it for a profit. I can't remember what life was like under the colonial or feudal regime; I was too small. Every household had to send one of its members to help build the post which was to house the French and their puppets. I went in place of my parents. The site was about half a mile away. I had to cart bricks and earth for the troops. My father used to relieve me when he could spare the time. We toiled for seven months, day in, day out, and afterwards we spent four or five months working on the roads. If I didn't report for duty, one of my brothers had to. We worked from six till eleven, stopping only for a cold snack which we had brought from home. They didn't give us anything to eat, and they didn't pay us. That was in 1951. The work of building the post went on for the whole of 1952. The French occupied the central post, with puppet troops all round them. These puppet troops were unarmed at the end of 1952. The local people didn't attack them at first because the Party hadn't yet established much of a following in the village. Late in 1952 the building work finally came to an end.

Round about June 1953 these posts were attacked by local guerrillas. One of the three puppet-manned posts was mined and blown up; the other two panicked and surrendered. Four months later, our forces attacked the main French post. The post was commanded by two Frenchmen and two Black Africans; otherwise it was completely manned by puppet troops. (Back in 1951 there had been two or three hundred Black Africans and about fifteen Frenchmen; but these had gradually been sent to other fronts and replaced by puppets.) We called on the puppet troops to surrender, but they wouldn't. So our regional forces and guerrillas got together and attacked them with mines and mortars. We kept up the loudspeaker appeals for a whole month, but they still wouldn't surrender. One night a couple of mines blasted the post wide open. They surrendered then, all right. There were fifty of them, including the two French lieutenants.

After the French pulled out, land reform began. At that time there were four landowners, including one reactionary who was a member of the puppet Council of Notables. He was put on trial and shot. The other three were allowed to work, but kept under house arrest. From 1954 till 1962 they had to appear in public once a month and listen to observations about their conduct. Today they are co-operators. The reactionary had owned seven maus, which wasn't much, but he had been guilty of crimes during his membership of the council. The other three had all owned about twenty maus. There was no need for any rehabilitations in the village, for no errors had been

committed. My own family obtained a small house from one of
the landowners, but it was so old that we simply used the material
to build another. We lived in that house from the time of the
land reform programme until 1962; it has been enlarged to
twice the size since then. We were given half a sao to use as an
allotment, and a mau and five saos for growing rice. My two
brothers were married, and I had to provide for my mother
and father and three children. Before we joined the co-operative
we had an annual surplus of rice (about twelve hundredweights),
and we usually sold two pigs. We had about twenty chickens
and a few geese. There was a big difference in our lives. We
used to market the surplus rice, and it brought in nearly
fourteen piastres a hundredweight – over 160 piastres a year.

I became a member of the co-operative after one harvest.
We didn't understand the new policy at first, and we were
greatly attached to our own property, but it wasn't long before
we joined. Up to that point, the family had owned a one-third
share in a buffalo, and our land was dotted about in half a
dozen different places. There were definite drawbacks in
staying out of the co-operative. You couldn't always plough
when you wanted to, for you had to wait till the buffalo was
free. Another thing: our bits and pieces of land lay right in the
middle of the collectively owned acres and were still unploughed
when the co-operative piped water in; we had to cross the
co-operative's paddy-fields to get to our own; the water in the
surrounding fields drained away our manure, and we weren't
allowed to make use of that water ourselves. So you see, staying
out of the co-operative made life very awkward for us – and
that is why we joined in 1960. Conditions have greatly improved
since then, and in 1966 we earned 8,000 points, in other words
forty-eight hundredweights of rice. We're a household of eight,
with four full-time workers. We keep pigs – three in all, including a sow – and this year they have earned us 220 dongs.
We keep poultry, too: we've earned eighteen dongs from geese
and forty-eight dongs from ducks. From our sales of surplus
rice and our whole range of production, we earned a total of
556 dongs in 1966. My earnings are above the local average.
Ploughing is my trade: I'm one of a team of six, and we have

half a dozen buffaloes. During 1966 I put in a total of 400 working days. Apart from ploughing, we collect duckweed for use as manure, and we earn extra points for helping with the damming and irrigation. All men and women between eighteen and forty-five have had to work an extra thirty-six days a year to pay for the services of the thirty-five skilled workers who look after the hydraulic side. Pregnant women are exempt, of course, and so are the sick. We do jobs like cleaning out the fish-ponds, shifting manure, and drying the paddy. I'm earning a good deal more than I did in the land reform days. Then there's my private allotment: I spend a little time on that after I've finished working in the fields.

There have been some changes in local life since the attacks started. Things like pots and pans are in short supply. And it's much the same with food. Before, we would breed three pigs, sell two and keep the third. Today we are only allowed to buy back twenty-six pounds of pork for every hundredweight we sell the state. Restrictions are tighter than they were, but it is our national duty to accept them.

Our aim is to drive the Americans out, so that we may be free to produce more . . .

2. The Province of Thai Binh

Vu Van Binh, permanent member of the Provincial Administrative Committee and Provincial Executive Committee of the Workers' Party:

This is the largest province in the delta. It is a storehouse of manpower and natural resources. The province covers an area of 580 square miles and has about 1,300,000 inhabitants. The density of population is 350 per square mile, setting aside the 300,000 inhabitants who have left for the highlands since the beginning of 1964. This movement of population is still going on. As far back as 1930, the peasants of Thien Hai rebelled in an attempt to secure the abolition of taxes. A number of people were killed during the rising in August 1945, and the famine led to a quarter of a million deaths in the province; some villages lost three quarters of their population. The French did not move into Thai Binh in strength until 1950. From 1945 till 1950 we had more or less total control of the province. Then they took up positions along the main highways, flanked the villages with forts, and proceeded to comb the area with their GMs [*groupes mobiles*]. Some of the villages actively engaged in the war were honeycombed with underground passages. We kept up the fight from 1950 till 1954. In May 1954, two months before the signing of the Geneva Agreements, the French pulled out of the province. When peace returned, we patched up our wounds and set about shaping the future.

In the old days, the landowners used to grab two thirds of whatever the peasants produced. In 1945 they were entitled to over four hundredweights per mau. We forced them to lower their ground rents by 25 per cent. In 1946 we set up People's Councils at local and provincial levels: 20,000 inhabitants elected a representative to the Provincial People's Council. Today we have 100 delegates on the Provincial Council, all elected at district level and representing the wishes of 640,000 inhabitants.

Administrative organization

The province of Thai Binh is made up of twelve districts, a provincial capital and 292 communes operating 700 co-opera-tives. Each district elects its own delegates: there are eight to eleven delegates per district, and three from the provincial capital. The People's Council meets twice a year. First of all, the delegates go out into the villages, for it is their job to convey the wishes and needs of the local people. Achievements are listed and discussed, and attention given to grass-root criticisms. Since 1966, we have set up People's Councils at district level, with forty to sixty delegates per district. The administrative machinery of the province operates as follows. . . . At the bottom end of the scale is the commune, electing its own Council of twenty to fifty members, who then choose seven, eight or nine of their own number to serve on the commune's Administrative Committee. Next comes the District People's Council: every village takes part in the election of between forty and sixty delegates; these in turn elect the District Administrative Council, which has nine to thirteen members. Finally there is the Provincial People's Council, whose delegates are chosen by the district electors. In Thai Binh, the Provincial Council is made up of 100 members, who are responsible for appointing the fifteen-member Provincial Administrative Committee. In short, the general population plays a direct part in choosing the delegates who sit on the People's Council, while the People's Council elects the Administrative Committee at each of the three levels. Any delegate can be dismissed before the end of his term of office. All are members of co-operatives and receive no pay except for the two annual meetings. This system has encouraged the masses to play an active role in the work of administration.

Production

In 1962, two districts – Quynh Coi and Phu Duc – reaped two tons an acre. Before that they had been only averagely successful districts. In 1966, eleven districts reached the level of two tons an acre. Today this figure has become the norm. Some districts have produced even more. There have been instances of 2.1 and even 2.2 tons. Four hundred and ten of the province's 700 co-operatives have exceeded two tons an acre. Two of them have achieved more than 2.8 tons an acre: the co-operative at Quang Nap (2.89) and the co-operative at Tan Phong (3.1). 95.5 per cent of the peasants are co-operators, and 92 per cent of the co-operatives are fully fledged. The people who are not yet members of co-operatives were previously landowners or rich peasants. We are in full possession of the facts about them, and they are accorded membership as and when their behaviour allows. We have been faced with problems over manpower and irrigation, but we've managed to solve them. Even small plots of land are kept supplied with water. We have hydraulic systems wherever they are needed, with complete equipment for supplying or draining moisture.

Technical Developments

The problem of manuring received careful attention in 1963–4. We laid 2.8 tons an acre. In 1966 we laid 5.6 tons an acre, and in places as much as 8.5 tons. Most of the manure came from piggeries. Alluvial water is supplied four times a year, and the water-level in the paddy-fields is a third of an inch higher. We have an unlimited supply of manure in the Red River; azolla is a very important element, too, and so is the use of lime.

There has been a considerable improvement in the quality of agricultural tools and machinery, thanks to the efforts of local industry. We now have a good rake for dealing with weeds – also the noria, which does the work of five full-time bailers. Fifteen per cent of our arable land is mechanized. We have a tractor depot and a repair centre in every district. But this is not enough: the situation still calls for a major effort. The American aggression began at the very moment when agriculture was crying out for more mechanization and the development of regional industry. Somehow we must continue to make progress in spite of the bombing, though the task is not an easy one.

Industries

We have a provincial industrial board, which has been de-centralized and moved to safety. The board is responsible to the Administrative Committee for the management of all industrial concerns within the province. There are five types of industry in Thai Binh: sugar refineries, paper mills, distilleries, pickling factories and silk works. Industries are sub-divided according to their particular functions, or grouped according to the nature of their raw materials. Alcohol, sugar and paper, for example, derive from a common raw material. Cane yields sugar; the waste-matter yields paper; the molasses yields alcohol. The managers and assistant managers are appointed by the state, while the workers make their own contribution to management via the management committees. There is a trade union to lay new schemes before the workers, so that the schemes may be debated and any useful suggestions adopted. The managerial staff are paid by the state, unlike the officials who run the farming co-operatives. Pay, of course, is determined on the basis of grade and output. There are four grades: apprentice, semi-skilled, skilled, highly skilled. Individual performances are assessed every three or six months, and workers can be either upgraded or downgraded. This method is well-suited to the training of technicians: they are able to win promotion while engaged in full-time work.

Dry and industrial crops

Dry crops – sweet potatoes, taros, maize – account for 10 per cent of all we grow. They have a high yield, representing 17 per cent of our income from agriculture, and their success enables us to develop our stock-farming interests. In Thai Binh we reap three harvests a year – two of rice, one of dry crops. The total area of arable land is on the increase, having risen from 469,000 acres to 518,000. Thus we are improving the living standards of the population and adding to the country's wealth. A dry-crop harvest can be extended to 40 per cent of our arable land. We expect to achieve this target in 1970.

Industrial crops are grown on 5 per cent of the arable land.

Among these are mulberries, to provide sustenance for silk-worms. In 1966 we produced sixty-five tons of natural silk, including fifty for export. In areas where we breed silkworms, the population is wealthy. By 1970 we expect to lift production to eighty tons. So long as the rice yield is in the region of two and a half tons an acre, land can be cleared for other crops.

We produce 7,000 tons of rushes, to supply raw material for mats and carpets, and four thousand tons of jute for the export market. Groundnuts are grown in conjunction with other crops over an area of 7,500 acres. Eighteen hundred and fifty acres are devoted to sugar-cane, and the yield is sufficient for the needs of local industry.

Then there is livestock and poultry. We sell 8,000 tons of pork to the state; this figure excludes the meat consumed by the local population, which accounts for about 30 per cent. We raise poultry, too, and sell a considerable quantity to the state canning industry. Most of the 500 tons of chicken is retained for local consumption, but we export 200 tons of duck. There are 50,000 oxen in Thai Binh. Every year we slaughter 3,000 which have outlived their time.

About a hundred communes make a handsome profit from fish-breeding, and we are planning a large-scale development in this sphere.

We are also planting a great many trees. We have no forests in Thai Binh. Fifty villages have planted orange and tangerine trees. The village of Thuan Vi, in the district of Thu Tri, produces 300 tons of oranges a year – an exceptionally high figure. In addition, there are 80,000 coconut palms in the province. These have an industrial use: the manufacture of soap. We propose to open a factory where we shall be able to can our own fruit and meat.

There are salt marshes along the coasts – 850 acres of them. We are about to clear a further 370 acres. In 1967 we obtained 1,200 tons of salt. The province is self-sufficient in this respect, and we are even able to set a quantity aside for industrial use. Ultimately we reckon to clear another 5,000 acres. In this area, the income from salt is higher than the income from rice.

We engage in deep-sea fishing, too. Generally we catch five or six thousand tons a year; but the war has created difficulties, and in 1967 we caught only 2,600 tons.

We have electric generating sets (10 kW) to deal with agricultural needs. There are 160 electrically operated pumps in Thai Binh, and 200 diesel pumps. Fifty villages have complete hydraulic systems. Two hundred and forty have to make do with systems which are only 30 to 50 per cent efficient. We hope to put this right by 1970. Only 12 per cent of the agricultural land is mechanized or semi-mechanized. Two hundred co-operatives have threshing machines and mechanical huskers.

Education

We have 9,000 third-phase pupils. Let me remind you that in the old days there were only 500 third-phase and 85,000 second-phase pupils in the whole of Indochina. Now we have 232 second-phase schools in this province alone. Each of our 292 villages contains a first-phase school. In all, we have 190,000 first-phase pupils and 90,000 children attending nursery or infant schools. There are adult classes in science and technology, held after working hours or in the middle of the day; these classes attract 120,000 students, who attend – on average – three times a week. In the old days, 90 per cent of the people could neither read nor write, but we have completely done away with illiteracy. Most of the agricultural workers have been educated up to Class 5 standard. We have come a long way in the field of technical education. We have crèches for 15,000 children between the ages of eight months and three years, which leaves their parents free to work.

Health services

Each district has its own hospital – making a total of twelve hospitals, each containing fifty to eighty beds. In the old days there used to be only one doctor to deal with the entire province. Now we have sixty-eight doctors, plus eight top-grade pharmacists and 550 medical auxiliaries. Two hundred and seventy of these medical auxiliaries are employed in the villages (serving 292 villages). Every village has two or three nurses. Eighty-five per cent of families own a dual-compartment septic tank. Throughout the province there is one well per six families, and each family has a small water-tank fitted with a filter.

A few facts and figures

Table 16. Average areas held by various peasant categories (in square yards)[1]

	Before land reform	After land reform
Hired labourers	229	1,119
Poor peasants	545	1,170
Average peasants	1,090	1,263
Rich peasants	3,014	1,377
Landowners	6,426	837

Table 17. Farming co-operatives.

	Total number of co-operatives	Socialist-type co-operatives	Semi-socialist co-operatives
1960	3,063	235	2,828
1962	1,758	534	1,224
1965	1,073	934	139
1966	777[2]	720	57

Table 18. Allocation of arable lands (in percentages).

Year	Rice	Other food crops
1957	95.7	4.3
1962	93.65	6.35
1965	89.22	10.78
1966	88.76	11.24

Table 19. Total agricultural production (in thousands of dongs).

	1960	1962	1965	1966
Total	140,320	153,930	172,500	174,737
Agriculture	131,413	146,715	173,258	186,509
Stock farming	25,574	29,728	33,155	29,663

1. Statistics supplied by the Provincial Administrative Committee and Party Committee.

2. Every year the co-operatives are regrouped into larger units.

Village Crèches

The crèche is housed in a modern building with a tiled roof. There are brick-lined shelters for use during air raids. On the tiled floor are four large beds, placed end to end and covered with matting. These, and the surrounding hammocks, are protected with mosquito nets.

The children – eighteen of them – are from three months to two years old. The monthly charge for keeping a child at the crèche is two dongs and six and a half pounds of rice.

The two girls who look after the children are remunerated in points, at the rate of nine points a day. They are in attendance on all but two days a month, when the crèche is closed for cleaning.

The children stay in the crèche from six in the morning until half-past five in the afternoon. They spend most of their time playing, eating and sleeping; but they are given a few simple exercises (lasting a total of ten minutes a day), and one of the girls in charge shows them how to sing and dance. They are also taught to speak. When I visited the building, we were greeted with cries of '*Chao Bac !*' ('Hullo, uncle!').

The children are washed thoroughly every morning; they have their own towels, which are supplied at a low fixed price. The Vietnamese traditionally adopt a casual attitude to toilet training: there is a vent in the children's shorts to provide for natural needs.

There are two meals a day, the first at nine in the morning (rice, fish soup, beans), the second (a similar meal, but sometimes including meat) at four in the afternoon. There is no milk. Before each meal, the utensils are immersed in boiling water, the flies are driven away, and the children's hands and feet are washed. The two girls in charge have attended a two-week course in hygiene and the prevention of diseases.

The doctor pays a brief call every day and makes a more thorough visit once a month, to check weights and measurements, etc.

To insure that the children are as well-fed as possible, the co-operative has donated an area of water for fish-breeding; every mother is expected to spend one day a month working at the ponds. In addition, the co-operative sold the crèche a hundredweight of rice in 1966.

There are seven such crèches within the co-operative.

A Village Medical Unit

This particular unit serves the needs of 5,558 inhabitants. The staff consists of a medical auxiliary, a woman pharmacist and two midwives. The unit has a dozen beds, with eight more in a place of safety. Electricity is laid on. Among the conditions dealt with are diarrhoea, pneumonia, colds, abscesses, simple fractures, childbirth (when there are no complications) and trachoma[3].

Medical inspections have been carried out by class, by hamlet and by neighbourhood. Ten cases of tuberculosis and three of leprosy were detected in 1966.

In 1967, second-stage vaccinations were given against poliomyelitis, tuberculosis, cholera, smallpox, tetanus and typhoid. Ninety-two per cent of the people have been vaccinated: a total of 5,126. The remainder, it is said, have chronic illnesses which make vaccination impossible.

Vaccinations against tetanus and tuberculosis are administered once every two years, and against smallpox once every five years. Vaccinations against cholera are administered annually.

In 1967, sixty-six births were registered. In 1966, eighty-four births were registered.

As for birth control, six women were sterilized in 1966 and sixteen in 1967. All were between the ages of thirty-five and forty-five, and all had borne at least four children.

The pharmacy is a large, scrupulously clean and tidy room containing sulphonamides, extraxycleme, vitamin B, aspirin, strychnine, vitamin C, streptomycin (stocks of this drug are renewed three times a month), penicillin and novocain.

3. I observed one case of trachoma, the victim being a year-old child.

The cases examined on 1, 3 and 4 November 1967 were as follows:

	Treatment given
Maxillary glands	Penicillin, Sulfathiazol
Angina of the throat	Penicillin, vitamin C
Rhonchus	Streptomycin, vitamin C
Cold	Traditional medicine, vitamin C and vitamin B1
Cough	Streptomycin, Broma, vitamin C
Infected white of eye	Penicillin, Sulfathiazol, eye-lotion
Bronchitis	Penicillin, Sulfathiazol, tonic syrup
Anaemia	Filaton (10 ampoules)

The Co-operative at Tan Phong

This is the best co-operative in North Vietnam. Established in 1959, it is now made up of 853 households comprising 4,112 persons. Seventy per cent of the 1,700 workers are women. The cultivated land extends over an area of 568 acres. By Vietnamese reckoning, the total productive acreage amounts to 1,530 acres, for two or three harvests are reaped from the same soil.

The co-operative grows rice and three industrial crops: mulberries, jute and groundnuts.

Table 20.

	Area (in maus)	1964	1966
Mulberries	15	10 cwt (of spun silk)	1 ton
Jute	10	18 cwt (of dried fibre, per mau)	1 ton
Groundnuts	250	8 cwt (of dried grain, per mau)	10 cwt

Table 21. Recent production figures for rice

	1964	1965	1966	1967
Tons per acre	2.2	2.7	2.9	1.5[4]

The total area devoted to rice is 500 maus.

Dry crops are grown, too. Table 22 shows the average yields per acre in 1964 and 1966.

Table 22.

	1964	1966
Maize	14 cwt	1.6 cwt[5]
Beans	8.6 cwt	10.8 cwt[6]
Sweet potato	6.5 tons	8.7 tons

4. This is the figure for the summer harvest only. The winter harvest was expected to yield 1.8 tons per acre, making a total of 3.3.

The co-operative adheres to a rigid system of crop rotation. In June the early (TH 2) rice is planted out. This is a dwarf rice, harvested in October and yielding 1.7 tons an acre. Immediately afterwards, a new variety of sweet potato is planted; harvested in February, it yields 4.3 tons an acre. Maize is cultivated in December, while the sweet potato is still growing, between the furrows. In February the sweet potato is harvested and the groundnuts are cultivated. The maize is harvested in May, the groundnuts in June, and the rice immediately afterwards. This rotational system is applied over an area of 135 acres.

Throughout the 182 acres of low-lying paddy-fields, there are two harvests a year, yielding 1.96 tons per acre per harvest. Half this area – i.e. ninety-one acres – is planted with A 10 rice and yields 3.36 tons per acre per year; the other is planted with A 10 (high) rice and yields 3.77 tons per acre per year.

Throughout the 274 acres of more elevated paddy-fields, there are three harvests: one of rice, one of maize, one of groundnuts.

The co-operative employs three agronomists and two Grade 2 technicians who deal with the problems of stock-farming. In addition, it is paying for the further education of a Grade 2 technician who will eventually become a fully qualified agricultural expert.

General facts about the co-operative

Total cultivated area	568 acres (about 600 maus)
Number of buffaloes	140
bullocks	20
pigs	270, including 26 sows[7]

5. There is only one maize crop, harvested midway between a groundnut crop and a bean crop.

6. The beans are planted at the foot of the maize.

7. In addition, there are 700 privately owned pigs. Poultry is privately owned, too. There is a grand total of about 8,000 birds and animals.

Food production per head is sixty-six pounds a month, including forty-six pounds of rice.

The accumulated funds of the co-operative amounted to 141,000 dongs in 1967. Expenditure for the year 1966 was 10,137 dongs, while capital as at 1 January 1967 was 474,507 dongs, a figure which included buffaloes, buildings, threshing-floors, etc., but which did not include the paddy-fields. Liquid assets, safely housed in the bank, are about 30,000 dongs. Only 500 dongs are kept in the co-operative's safe.

There is electric power for use in the schools and at the medical unit, as well as for pumping purposes.

The co-operative is mechanized, or at least semi-mechanized, owning two pumping stations, three diesel engines, a husker, a mechanical mixer (for preparing pig-swill) and a threshing machine.

The household which earned the highest number of points in 1966 received 3.5 tons of rice. This was a family of six, including four full-time workers. Their financial income is shown in Table 23.

Table 23.

Pigs	300 dongs
Poultry	100 dongs
Fruit and vegetables	100 dongs
Surplus rice (1.4 tons)	600 dongs
	1,100 dongs

The household with the lowest number of points (a family of four, including two full-time workers) received 1.6 tons of rice. Their financial income is shown in Table 24.

Table 24.

Pigs	300 dongs
Poultry	50 dongs
Fruit and vegetables	20 dongs
Surplus rice (6 cwt)	135 dongs
	505 dongs

Bui Thi Tinh, aged twenty-two. She has been a Party member for the past two years and is vice-chairwoman of the Administrative Committee. She is one of seven children; her parents are poor peasants. She has been educated to Class 7 standard and would like to work her way up to Class 10:

In the old days it was the husband who was educated and took all the decisions, while the wife remained untaught. Even today there are mothers who cannot read, but they play their part in the running of family affairs and talk things over with their husbands, on an equal footing. Distinctions are no longer drawn between members of the same family: children of both sexes are sent to school; girls are equally free to join in discussions on social affairs; even in combat units, there is no discrimination – for women are just as capable of shooting at aircraft. Ploughing used to be regarded as a man's job; but today, in response to the Three Tasks campaign[8], we have learned to handle the plough ourselves. Six of the seven girls in our production team, for instance, can plough as well as anyone. We have even done night work, collecting sludge for use in making manure: that's another job which only men used to do.

Women get the same pay as men and enjoy additional advantages. They are allowed three rest days a month, during menstruation, and get a month off – with full pay – before and after the birth of each child. A mother who cannot properly breast-feed her baby is given eight tins of condensed milk; she also gets four and a half pounds of sugar, three yards of clothing material, and some meat coupons for her own use. That applies to women working in the administrative departments. Peasant women are entitled to two or three months' rest when they give birth to a child; the co-operative provides them with forty-four pounds of rice, three yards of clothing material (i.e. the full annual quota for people living in the country; townspeople get five) and four and a half pounds of sugar.

8. The 'Three Tasks' are as follows: (a) take over all jobs previously reserved for men; (b) deal with all household tasks; (c) play an active part on all fronts (production, social affairs, military).

Every co-operator has to devote fifty working days a year to collective tasks which will benefit the state or the co-operative; usually these tasks are connected with damming and irrigation. Expectant and nursing mothers are exempt from such duties. If a pregnant woman is short of rice, the co-operative sells her some at a special reduced rate. Young mothers are given easy jobs, and women who have suffered a miscarriage are entitled to the same benefits.

There are adult education classes for women, giving them a detailed knowledge of agriculture and other subjects, so that they can play a full and well-informed role in all forms of social activity. Today we have girls of eighteen or nineteen running schools, or supervising production teams, or serving on the co-operative's management committee.

Four of the girls in my own team, for instance, hold fairly responsible positions. One is on the management committee; another is head of the team; the third looks after the team's accounts; the fourth is head of a women's group in the Young Workers.

When one speaks of a 'peasant', it is important to bear in mind that nowadays she is usually a woman of many roles. She is a producer, a housewife, a technician and a combatant.

Since the attacks started, I have really come to hate the American aggressors. I have tried to convert my hatred into physical energy. I believe the rest of the women share my feelings.

We were working within a mile of Thai Binh, our provincial capital, when the Americans raided it in December 1966. They destroyed nearly every building in the town. We ran for shelter. Mud was flying all over the place. After the raid, we worked on until six o'clock. Usually we stop at about five. But that day we were all of one mind: we would work longer and harder. Afterwards we were awarded two extra points for courage and efficiency.

What is socialism?
– It lies in the fact that Party and state are striving hard to improve the social, economic and cultural life of the community.

- The citizens of a socialist country are multi-skilled workers, all making their contribution to the building of socialism.
- Everyone enjoys the fruits of his labours, and everyone is rewarded according to the work he or she does. Nobody can exploit us or grab what is ours.

The Slaughter of Dai Lai

I arrived in Thai Binh province on 3 November 1967. Dai Lai had been bombed the day before, and at my request the local authorities took me to see the damage. We reached the village at dawn on 4 November, forty hours after the attack.

I must first point out that the province has suffered only light bombing compared with the country as a whole. It contains very few targets which anyone could term strategic. Indeed, it is exclusively agricultural and its uniformly flat and unwooded terrain makes concealment all but impossible.

Nevertheless, the US Air Force attacked the province 230 times between early 1965 and the end of 1966, and – again according to the local authorities – 491 times between 1 January and 31 October 1967. The provincial capital was bombed in 1966 and, as I saw for myself, almost completely destroyed. The dikes, of capital importance in the delta region, where they stave off flooding and drought, have been attacked forty times. No less than a third of the raids have inflicted loss and suffering on the civilian population.

I was not given the total number of casualties, for this is regarded as a military secret. But I was told, for instance, that fifty people were killed in the raid on the hamlet of Phong Man (May 1966), and thirty in the attack on the second-phase school in the village of Thuy Dan (October 1966).

Dai Lai was the third village I had seen lying devastated after an American attack. On 9 October, Olivier Todd and I had visited Tuy Hoi, in the district of Gia Vien. The raid, carried out at 12.30 a.m. the previous day, had killed seven and injured eight. There was nothing remotely resembling a strategic target for miles around, not even an anti-aircraft gun. The second raided village I had seen was Kim Bai, in the district of Thanh Hoa, where on 26 October several waves of

aircraft had destroyed about twenty solidly constructed buildings, including a pharmacy and a children's nursery. I arrived
in the village on 29 October. The raid had killed seventeen
civilians and wounded twenty-two more. I should like to point
out that my tour was confined to the area north of the twentieth
parallel; most of my time was spent in the Red River delta,
which is far from being the worst-hit region.

So the attack on Dai Lai was not an isolated occurrence.
There are no strategic targets of any kind in the vicinity of
the village. It lies midway between two branches of river, about
half a mile from the provincial highway, over three miles from
the nearest bridge, in a flat landscape of canals, paddy-fields
and pools. I did not see a single anti-aircraft gun in the area.

Two American planes were involved in the attack. Visibility
was good. There can be no question of ascribing what happened to a technical error, or of arguing that the bombs were
dropped to lighten a crippled plane limping back to base.

It was early morning when we reached the village. Some of
the ashes were still warm. Men and women were busy clearing
away the rubble. The two aircraft had dropped sticks of
incendiaries and high-explosives. Witnesses were all agreed
that there had been at least fifteen explosions. The attack
occurred at 1 p.m. on 2 November, killing fifty-one people
and injuring thirty-nine. The total population of the village
was 255. Out of forty-one families, thirty-four were rendered
homeless. Scarcely a house escaped total destruction or serious
damage.

Men were weeping silently. A girl, flanked and comforted
by two old women, was wailing aloud. Another was crying as
she swept debris from the foundations of a missing house. She
burst into tears as we passed. 'He couldn't get out because of
the heat,' she sobbed. 'I could see his arms jutting from the
flames.'

At the time of the attack most of the peasants were out in
the fields, reaping the tenth-month harvest. A few were at

work in the village, husking the rice. As soon as the planes were heard, they all raced to the trenches or the individual dugouts. The children took to the indoor shelters at the sound of the first explosion. A few of the houses were felled by blast; others had their thatch roofs set alight by incendiaries. The blaze spread through the village, making rescue difficult; but the militia managed to save a few. Charred bodies were found in the shelters; the heat had burst their flesh. Some were so badly shattered and mangled that identification was impossible. Of the fifty-one victims, thirty-nine were less than fifteen years old.

Bui Thi Tinh[9], who supervised the task of identification and burial, told me:

I was about half a mile from the village. From my dugout I could see two planes, one flying lower than the other. The low-flying plane was the first to drop its bombs. It happened after the midday meal. Some of the workers were already in the fields, others were on the point of setting out. The children and old people were having their siesta. I counted sixteen bombs, falling in a single stick. Huge flames rose from the village, shooting high as the treetops. The planes dropped their bombs and flew away. It all happened very quickly. Then the militia moved in, without a moment's delay, and people raced to the scene with buckets, ropes and spades. They tried to put the fire out, drawing water from the ponds and forming a human chain. They fought their way through to the trenches at the heart of the fire. The earth had fallen in, so some of them began to dig the survivors out. A gust of wind made the fire spread quicker than ever. A number of the rescuers were burned alive. A co-operator from one of the neighbouring villages, a man named Them, saved seven people by his own efforts; he ran back and forth, back and forth, carrying them on his back. A worker named Roan had left four children at home. As he hurried back to them, shrapnel sliced his body in four.

I started running towards the village in the company of three

9. See page 177.

other girls. I had some gauze and cotton wool in my bag, and I handed these to comrades. As we ran, we saw what looked like a human body buried under a pile of straw. We went over to where it was lying, meaning to pull the man clear, but we found there was nothing left except the two legs: the upper part of the body had been carried away by blast. There were flames everywhere, and really thick smoke. You couldn't see more than five or six yards in front of you. The heat was intense. There were a great many of us, and we were all pushing and shoving in our efforts to help. The threshing-floor was strewn with blood and bodies. By this time, the wounded had been carried away on stretchers. I had shed my sandals, and the ground was so hot it was burning my feet. The workers had darted back from the fields as soon as the planes had gone. Some of them were sobbing and shrieking amid the flames, and yet they still tried to put the fire out. Roan's wife wanted to hurl herself into the blaze, in a bid to save her children; she had just seen her husband blown to pieces before her eyes. When the others sought to restrain her, she started tearing her clothes like a madwoman. She flung herself upon me, shouting: 'Help me get in! Help me get in!' 'If you love me,' I said, 'you must come with me.' At this, she said: 'Why should I? Who am I to live with? They're all dead.' She kept on saying the same thing: 'Who am I to live with? Who am I to live with?' And once again she tried to hurl herself into the blaze. 'You will live with us,' I said. And we dragged her away.

I saw the five Ru children lying dead in the same trench as their mother; they were among the first to be dug out . . . Nguu and his wife were in the fields. One of their children happened to be away from the village. The other four were all killed: there was nothing left of the eldest boy but his trunk and his left leg. . . . The next house contained a family of four. The man and wife were in the fields, but their two children were killed. . . . Another co-operator, a man named Khoi, lost his whole family: his two children; his wife, who was expecting a third in a month's time; and his mother, whose body was blown into the branches of a tree – when we found her, her blood was trickling down the bark.

When at last the fire was out, I stayed behind to see that the bodies were properly prepared for burial. The state shop supplied four yards of material per coffin. It was half-past two when we started grouping the bodies. I saw things that made me physically sick. Some of the bodies were so badly burnt that there was nothing left of them except the skin stretched tight over the bones, with the guts spilling out of the burst bellies; they had become objects without human shape. We collected all the bits and pieces: arms, legs. . . . Sometimes a tuft of hair would show that the victim was a woman. I entered the names of the deceased in the register, and some of my comrades painted the probable ages or identities on small signboards so that these could be placed on the graves. A number of bodies were beyond identification: we assessed the ages by the size of the feet, marking the coffins 'four-year-old child', 'ten-year-old child', and so on.

Among these human scraps, I saw a heap of flesh which – judging by the tuft of hair and also the bust – seemed to be a girl of about fifteen. It was terrible to see a length of thigh, still rounded and golden, somehow attached to this pulp. The charred bodies of some of the children looked more like stunted dogs.

Tran Thi Sai, aged thirty:

I lost my father when I was twelve, and my mother has just been killed in this air raid. My husband's family died of starvation in 1945. He and his young sister were all I had left, and now he is gone too. My family were 'average peasants'. Our house covered slightly less than a sao, and we had five saos of rice-growing land. When the French moved their forces into the area, we had to do forced labour for them and help them build their post. I was thirteen or fourteen at the time. Afterwards we took jobs on other people's estates, for we did not own enough land to make a living from it. I didn't have any brothers – just an elder sister. There was no chance of our going to school. We helped on the land and went crab-hunting.

Under the land reform programme, we kept the land we already owned but did not receive any extra. There used to be two big landowners in the area: they and their families fled to the South. We had to fend for ourselves – just my mother and us two girls. I got married when I was eighteen. My husband came from a family of landless peasants. His parents had died of starvation in 1945, and of their five children only two were left. He was allotted three saos of rice-land. He was twenty when we married. We didn't have any surplus rice; indeed, we hadn't enough for our own needs. We used to catch fish and crabs, take them to market and use the profit to buy the rice we were short of. We gradually built up a stock, but we never had much.

We lost no time in joining the co-operative, for conditions were hard by then. We answered the call in the very first year. As a result, we obtained four hundredweights of rice for our own consumption – just enough to feed us. We didn't have a surplus at the end of the second year either. Not until the third year did we get an extra two hundredweights of rice. That was in 1962. Since then, we have always received about two hundred-weights of surplus rice – sometimes a bit more, sometimes a bit less. Last year (1966) our household, with two full-time workers, achieved 3,000 points; our earnings were 150 dongs. There were seven of us in all: myself, my husband, my mother and my four children . . .

At the time of the air raid I was with friends. We were on our way to the fields, where we expected to spend the afternoon bringing in the harvest. When I heard the planes, I took shelter in a dugout. As soon as the bombs had fallen, I ran home to see what had happened. Even from a distance, I could see that the whole village was ablaze. I took off my yoke and flung it aside so as to get along quicker. My second child – a boy – managed to escape from the fire. His little brother, aged five, tried to follow him but couldn't keep up; he got trapped in the courtyard. My mother picked up my twelve-month-old baby and tried to dash from the building: they were burnt alive in the doorway. My ten-year-old daughter was out minding the buffalo, so she was spared. My husband was a foreman. He and his team were husking rice, right here in the village. He stayed in the open till the very end, to make sure the others got into the shelter. That was how he came to be killed. The shrapnel split his head open. I stood screaming and sobbing while some of the other workers rushed into the flames in an attempt to save their families. I tried to do the same: hurl myself into the blaze and rescue my mother and children. But I was stopped and led away so that I shouldn't see their bodies as they were brought out.

I lost my mother, the baby she held in her arms, my five-year-old son and my husband. There are only three of us left: my two children and myself.

Bui Van Nguu, aged forty-six:

My parents were poor peasants. By the time I was fourteen I was living and working in the city, corking bottles in a distillery. My elder sister was still living at home with my mother, who was already a widow. When I was seventeen, my mother asked me to come back to the village. I became a ploughman on the estate of a wealthy landowner. I continued in his service for seven or eight years. The wage was six or seven piastres a year, payable in advance, plus food and clothing. In 1945 my mother died of starvation.

I got married when I was twenty-three or twenty-four. I found employment within my wife's family, for her aunt – who was also her foster-mother – had no son and asked me to stay with them. They were a family of 'average peasants'. When the revolution broke out, my wife's aunt gave us a house and seven saos of rice-land. But when the French returned to the village and set up the Council of Notables, she took the land back and sent us packing. When peace returned, we managed to buy a small plot (seventy-five square yards) and a three-room cottage.

The value of the plot was put at 200 dongs. I paid in rice – ten hundredweights for land and house together. In 1955 my wife's aunt – the one who had sent us packing – was unable to recruit enough labour for her paddy-fields. She asked us to return. I spent the next six months working for her; but she wasn't satisfied, so she threw us out again.

Under the land reform programme, I was classified as a poor peasant and given seven saos of land. I had three children by that time: two boys and a girl. Later I joined the co-operative.

Once the programme got under way, I had eight hundredweights of surplus rice a year. I worked on my own plot and on plots belonging to other peasants. Before collective farming began, I used to take rice to the provincial capital and sell it at market. With the proceeds I could afford to buy quite a few of the things we needed: three beds, for instance, and a pair of mosquito nets. Also, I was able to build a threshing-floor and a water tank. I joined the co-operative at a time when there was no work available, apart from looking after my own plot. I also joined because I love socialism and the idea of reunification. Each year has brought us another step forward. In 1966 (we were a family of seven by then, having had two more children in the meantime) we earned 7,000 points. In addition to two hundredweights – or just over – of surplus rice, we received 800 dongs from the sale of poultry and livestock and from payments for looking after the co-operative's buffalo.

At the time of the air raid I was at home, making brooms for the co-operative. My two daughters were in the kitchen, opposite where I was working. They were busy with the pestle and mortar. Their two small brothers were in the kitchen with them, playing games. My wife had left our youngest child, a girl of eighteen months, asleep in the hammock while she went to do some washing at the pond.

When my wife saw the planes coming, she started running towards the house; but before she could get back, she was blown off her feet by the blast of a bomb. Another high-explosive hit the kitchen, burying our four children. And then the house collapsed and caught fire. The roof fell in on me. The baby girl in the hammock started to cry. I scrambled up and caught her in my arms, and ran through the flames with her. When we got to the yard I saw my wife lying flat on the ground, half buried beneath the remains of the wall. She called out to me. I put the baby in the dugout and went to her aid. By the time I reached her, she was trying to get up of her own accord. Her clothes were badly torn and her face was bleeding. I handed the baby to her and told her to carry it to safety. Then I hurried off and tried to free my other four children.

I searched among the debris. I could only piece three of their bodies together. There was no trace of my eldest daughter. I didn't find her body until yesterday morning: it had been blown into an allotment about thirty feet away. It was buried under a pile of ashes. I would never have found her if I hadn't had others to help me. At first we thought it was someone else, but I looked and there could be no mistaking the shape of her ear. She was thirteen.

Hoang Ban, aged forty-four:

I was one of seven children, my mother being the second of my father's two wives. He had two wives because it seemed his first wife was not going to bear him any children. But after his second marriage, she began to conceive; which is why my two big sisters, born of the same mother as me, were older than my senior brothers[10].

When I was three, my father held the post of village constable. He was beaten by the elders, and the beating made him so ill that he died. We were all very poor after his death. In 1940, one of the sons by the first wife died. I took work as a hired labourer, ploughing for wealthy landowners, and the other brothers did the same. In 1945 we were allotted some paddy-fields, on a temporary basis. My household owned three saos of common land. We had to carry on working as ploughmen: it was the only way we could make a living. My sisters were married by that time and living elsewhere. There were only six of us left: my mother and my four brothers. We clubbed together and bought an ox. But one of my brothers and I were suspected of being political cadres – which wasn't true – and we had to move out of the village. That was in the days of the

10. Children by the first wife always enjoy seniority, even if they are younger in years.

French occupation; there were military posts everywhere. My other three brothers were left in peace and got on with the ploughing. In 1954 the French forces pulled out of Thai Binh, and I returned to my village.

I married in 1946. My eldest boy was born in 1947. I've had four children so far. My brother – the one who was killed the day before yesterday – had four children too.

After the land reform measures of 1956, my household owned a total of a mau and a half; that's taking the old and new plots together. Previously we had only had three saos. My brother and his family received 1.3 maus in all. I bought another plot from my neighbour, to enlarge those I already held. My brother and I were given a half-share in a buffalo, while my other brothers kept the bullock we had all bought between us. In 1960 we joined the co-operative; we were in the second wave of members. Since then, I have worked in one production team and my brother in another.

There was no chance of a rice surplus until 1965. Up to then, we received just enough for our own needs. In 1966 I sold 3.6 hundredweights to the state, and my brother 3.2. And after the first harvest this year he sold two hundredweights and I sold 1.4. My brother had about four hundredweights of rice at home: it didn't get burnt, it just got covered with earth. My own rice was unharmed, for my house was one of the few to escape damage. It is solidly built, with a thatch roof, whereas my brother's was made of wood.

At the time of the raid I was on my way to the fields with some of the workers; we expected to spend the afternoon bringing in the harvest. I heard the planes, but though I looked I couldn't see them. Then suddenly I heard a series of explosions and saw our village ablaze. We were about half a mile away. We ran back as fast as we could, but by the time we got there the whole village was ringed with flames.

My sister-in-law had come rushing back from the fields, just like me. When I saw her, she had her two-year-old son in her arms. His head was shattered. She cried out to me, asking me to go and help rescue her other children. My house is 400 yards from my brother's, and I ran all the way. It hadn't burnt down: it had been blown to bits. There was nothing left of the roof or walls. I made straight for the indoor shelter – a dugout with a lid over it, situated under the bed. Lying on the edge of this dugout was half the body of my two-year-old niece. I picked it up, carried it into the yard and went back to the dugout to search for the others. I pulled out the body of my brother's ten-year-old daughter. The lid of the shelter had disintegrated and smashed her head open. One of her arms was broken and her body was black all over. I carried her into the yard and shouted for help. Some members of the militia came to my assistance, and other people too. We brought out the body of the eight-year-old girl. Her head had been smashed like her sister's, and she had a broken leg. Afterwards we managed to dig out two other little girls, both aged five. These were other nieces of mine, who had come to the house to play with their cousins. They had died of suffocation. Six children, all dead . . .

We found bits and pieces of my brother. His arms and legs were in the kitchen. His insides were sticking to the bamboo wall. We recovered his ribs and breastbone, but not his head.

His wife is the only survivor, and it is as though she were out of her mind. She's living with us now. She keeps on sobbing and screaming, and no one can get through to her.

Phan Thi Nan, aged thirty-two:

I come from a family of poor peasants. My father used to work on a landowner's estate, and my mother was in service with another landowning family. I lost my father when I was five; my mother is still with us. From the time my father died till the time I was eight I acted as nursemaid to the land-owner's child. Then my mother and I left the landowner's house and tried to earn a living on our own. We received a small wage for minding oxen belonging to wealthy local peasants.

In 1950 the French reoccupied the village. I got wounded by a shell while I was planting rice. A piece of shrapnel caught me in the thigh, and I've walked with a limp ever since. In those days I found it hard to make enough to live on, and the village was often raided. I got married round about 1954. My husband was a poor peasant too. We received a temporary grant of about six saos, and under the land reform programme we were given a mau of rice-land and a quarter-share in a buffalo. We could afford to buy a bed and build a small bamboo house. We had enough rice to keep us going, but none to spare.

After land reform, we started getting two hundredweights of surplus rice a year. We had our first child about a year after we married, and until the air raid I had six children in all – one boy and five girls. The oldest was twelve, the youngest only a year. We joined the collective farming scheme in the very first year – that was in 1959. We received only two hundredweights of surplus rice. This was less than the year before, but the position was explained to us and we were promised that things would soon pick up. Sure enough, we received three hundredweights in the second year. We were able to buy a mosquito net and a blanket. We bred our own pigs and poultry: today we have three pigs and 200 birds. By 1963 we could afford to build a brick house with a paved yard and a water tank.

I was working in the fields when it happened. I looked up and saw two planes dropping bombs. At the sight of the smoke and flames rising from the hamlet, I ran home as fast as I could. As I approached my own house, I could see it was on fire. There was no sign of my children, and I thought they must all be inside. I sobbed and screamed and shouted for help. People heard me and came to my assistance. My husband had been working in the fields like me. He came rushing back too and he was shouting just as I was. He hurled himself into the flames, hoping to save the children. He got burnt, though not too badly. He is in hospital now, having treatment. My eldest child was down at the river, and one of my daughters was playing in the yard. The blast flung her into the village street. She was injured, but at least she's alive. Two of the others – the four-year-old and the eleven-year-old – were in the next house, so they escaped as well. But my two youngest – one was three, the other twelve months – were in the house.

They were badly charred when we found them. Their hands

were clenched tight, and black from burning. Their bodies had cracked open in places, and their insides were spilling from their bellies. The other villagers wrapped the two children and placed them in coffins, and then they were buried. I remained with them until the very last moment, for I did not want to lose sight of them.

Pui Thi Ru, aged fifty-one:

Both my grandfather and my father were very poor. My father was a landless peasant. By the time I was six I was employed as nursemaid to a landowner's daughter. I remained in service with the same family until I was fifteen. At sixteen I married and moved in with my husband's family: they were poor peasants. He and I did jobs for landowners and rich peasants. Within three years of marrying him, I had two daughters. We had very little to eat. In 1945 my husband and two daughters starved to death during the great famine. I was left all alone in the world and had to wander round the neighbouring villages, begging for food. In 1947 I married again. My second husband was a poor peasant too. We rented a room in a neighbour's house and worked for one of the local landowners. In 1948 we received a temporary grant of three saos.

In 1950 the French reoccupied the province. They kept raiding and searching the villages, and we had a very hard time of it. Later on, I had two more children. My eldest boy is sixteen, and my second eldest ten. The youngest was eight. He died the day before yesterday. Under the land reform programme we received six saos and a quarter-share in a buffalo. Life became a little easier. We joined the co-operative during the second phase, at the end of 1960. I was a nursing mother at the time, so I couldn't do my share of the work. The co-operative didn't give us any extra rice the first year, whereas in 1958 and 1959 we had achieved a surplus. We had barely enough to live on. Since 1962, though, we have been collecting a surplus of three hundredweights a year. In 1963 we built a wooden house and bought a bed and a mosquito net. The co-operative provided us with bricks and cement so that we could make our own well and a dual-compartment septic tank. Last year we received 4.6 hundredweights of rice; we reared two pigs and ten or a dozen birds and planted tea in the allotment. My husband died last year.

I was in the sweet-potato field at the time of the raid. I heard planes in the sky, and as I glanced up I saw two of them flying over the hamlet. Then I heard a number of explosions and saw flames and smoke over the houses. I hurried home. I saw my eldest son standing in the yard. 'Where are your two brothers?' I asked. 'One of them couldn't be got out,' he said; 'he was in the bedroom, and he's dead by now.' The boy he was speaking of was the youngest, and I cried. We couldn't get into the house because of the heat and flames. As soon as the fire had been put out, I went inside and found him. His body was black all over. His belly had burst open, and so had his knees. At the time of the attack, the eldest boy had been drying some straw on the threshing-floor. When he saw the planes he collected his younger brother, who was playing in the yard, and put him under cover. A moment later the house caught fire, and the child was cut off. I went to his funeral at half-past five today.

Losing my son has hurt me terribly. It comes very hard on us, being bombed like this when we are helpless to do anything. I'm eager for vengeance, and that is why I should like you to write about all this. We were living quietly and peacefully in our own village, and yet we were treated to a savage attack.

Bui Van Xuoc, aged thirty-six:

My parents were very poor. We had no cropland and no paddy-fields. I became an orphan at the age of thirteen – both my parents died of starvation in 1945. I owe my life to my aunt, who fed me during the famine. Afterwards I worked for one of the local landowners and remained in his employment until 1948. I earned my own living and lived with my aunt. I used to go fishing, too, and catch crabs and snails; I would take these things to market and sell them.

I got married in 1950. Both of us worked, and we lived with

my mother-in-law. The French reoccupied the province, and my house was burnt down during the mopping-up operations at the end of 1950. At that point my wife and I were hard put to it to earn a living. It wasn't until 1954 that we could afford to build a small bamboo house of our own. Late in 1955 we were given a temporary grant of rice-growing land: four saos of paddy-fields. Our first son was born in 1952, and our second in 1955. We had a third son in 1960 and a daughter in 1965. Three boys and one girl.

Under the land reform programme we received another four saos, making eight in all, and a quarter-share in a buffalo. In 1958 we built a large, three-room bamboo house. We worked as a team and made a profit from pigs and poultry. We had two pigs and about twenty birds, and every four months we used to go to market and put some up for sale. The pigs earned us over 200 dongs, and the poultry over 100. I had an allotment too. In addition, I used to earn a bit of extra money by carrying goods for a nearby shop. I was among the first to join the collective farming scheme in 1959. I was told that I had been living in appalling conditions ever since I was a child, and that things had improved under the Party. This was the plain truth. So when I was asked to give the co-operative a try, I gave it a try. Most peasants were unhappy about joining the co-operative, and many of them were determined to keep a weather eye open. In the first two years, the yields were poor. It wasn't until 1963 that I received 1.2 hundredweights of surplus rice. In 1964 we received two hundredweights, and in 1965 we received the same – even though my wife was busy with the new baby. In 1966 we again received two hundredweights. I was still breeding two pigs a year, and in 1966 I bred more poultry than ever before. My wife and I earned 6,200 points between us. We ate well, and we earned 405 extra dongs.

We had finished lunch and were about to return to the fields when we heard the sound of aircraft engines and the roar of exploding bombs. I was at home. I didn't even have time to get to the shelter: I just flung myself flat on the floor. I could see flames and smoke at the other end of the village, and I realized that the bombs must have fallen near my mother-in-law's house. I got up and started running towards it. Hers was the end house, and it was in flames. My wife's brother had escaped, followed by his son; but suddenly the blaze had spread to the whole house, and the walls had collapsed. We did our best to fight the fire, and when it was out we searched among the ruins and found the charred bodies of my mother-in-law and my wife's young sister. My mother-in-law's neighbour was in the shelter with them. She had been expecting a child in two months' time; now she was dead and her body, like theirs, was broken and black from burning. After we got them out from the shelter, they were put in coffins – at about five in the afternoon – and buried that same day.

Every time I look at my wife I think of my mother-in-law and sister-in-law, and I say to myself: 'How can they possibly do such things?'

I visited the central hospital and spoke to some of the casualties from the raid on Dai Lai.

Nguyen Thi Thang, aged forty-six:

I was working on the drying-floor when it happened. I didn't have time to get to the shelter. I don't remember anything else. All I remember is that the drying-floor was crowded.

Medical diagnosis: Deep back wound, with metallic fragments in the chest. Operation to be performed tomorrow. The patient has been given dry plasma to improve her general condition, together with sulpha drugs and penicillin. One of her children, aged seven, was killed in the same air raid. She has not been informed yet.

Nguyen Hop Thanh, aged forty-six:

I was on my way to the fields, to help with the harvest. I was alone, for I was a bit late. Suddenly I heard planes. They were flying very high, though, and I couldn't see how many there were. Then I heard a series of really loud roars and saw flames shooting high above the hamlet. There were no dugouts or trenches near, so I dumped my yoke and buckets and flung myself flat on the roadway. I passed out and don't remember anything after that. I'm told my mouth was pouring with blood, and even now I bring up a clot whenever I spit.

Medical diagnosis: Chest wound. The X-ray shows a piece of shrapnel in the left lung. An operation will be carried out as soon as the patient's general state of health improves. He has a haemoptysical condition: the shrapnel has traversed the pleura and injured the lung.

Nguyen Nge Dien, aged twelve. The following account was given by his father, who was at the boy's bedside:

At five past one he was getting ready to go to school. He was in the yard, with his books and belongings under his arm. When he saw the planes, he threw himself flat; he didn't have time to get to the shelter. The bomb exploded within twenty feet of him. As soon as the raid was over, I hurried home. The whole house was ablaze. I saw this boy lying in the middle of the yard. His two brothers were about thirty yards away, in the corner of the allotment. The youngest was treated at the district infirmary, for he wasn't seriously hurt – just a small wound over the arm. My other son received a slight injury to his left hand, and he was treated at the district infirmary too. Both of them have now been discharged. But this boy was wounded in six places. The two most serious wounds are in the head and belly. When I found him, he was unconscious and covered with blood. His clothes were ripped to pieces.

I took my vest off and tore it to make a dressing for his head and stomach. A few moments later, members of the anti-aircraft defence committee came and took him away to the first-aid post. My wife had taken shelter in a trench in the corner of the yard. She was still in the trench when I found her, having fainted from fear.

Medical diagnosis: This boy has a perforating wound in the

abdomen. He underwent a preliminary operation at the district hospital on the morning of 4 November 1967; the hollow parts of the intestine were stitched up. In addition, he had an open cranio-encephalic wound. A further operation was performed here, to remove the shrapnel and pieces of broken bone. He has lost a great deal of blood. This patient is suffering from infectious encephalitis. His condition is very grave.

Nguyen Thi Rinh, aged forty:

I was with the production team at the time. We were on our way to the fields, to bring in the harvest. When I reached the edge of the village, I saw some planes approaching. I had a clear view of them as they bombed the hamlet. The flames shot up at once. I didn't have time to find a dugout. I flung myself flat on the ground beside the pool. A piece of shrapnel hit me in the neck, and the blood came pouring out. I screamed for help. I heard the others say: 'There's no point. She'll die anyway, after losing all that blood. We'd do better to help the others.' So I lay there for over an hour, until I couldn't cry out any more; in the end I was surrounded by a pool of congealing blood. I was driven away on a lorry, and afterwards I was taken to the district infirmary, where my wounds were dressed. As my condition was serious, I was transferred to this hospital at ten o'clock the same night. Every so often I passed out. I wasn't unconscious all the time, but I felt really ill. My family came to see me. They talked to me, but I couldn't hear a word they said.

Medical diagnosis: Neck wound, with bomb splinters near the carotid artery. Due to be operated on tomorrow.

Trinh Thi Men, aged thirteen:

I was in the kitchen, cooking some beans. My mother was drying rice in the yard, and my sick father was in bed. My little sister was resting beside him. My young brother had gone out to play. I stepped outside the kitchen door and met an elderly neighbour who was going by. 'Did you see the plane?'

he asked. 'Yes,' I said, 'I did.' And a moment later the bombs exploded. The blast knocked me flat on my face in the yard, and a pile of thatch blew down from the roofs and covered me over. Blood poured from my neck, and I thought it was coming from my mouth. There was no one to help me, and I was screaming from pain and fear. I tried to pop my head out of the pile of thatch. By luck my uncle saw me and hurried over. He lifted me out and held me in his arms. 'Can it be you?' he asked. He carried me to the far end of the village. There he laid me down, and an orderly dressed my wound. Afterwards my uncles took me on a stretcher to the local first-aid unit.

There were no nurses or orderlies available at the first-aid unit, so I was sent on to the district infirmary. It was still light when I got there. They changed my dressing and gave me some injections, then they put me in a car and brought me here. It was dark by that time. I could see stars in the sky. I don't remember anything after that.

Medical diagnosis: Wound on the left side of the neck. Operation carried out on 2 November 1967. The sterno-scleno-mastoid muscle (controlling the movements of the neck) and the trapezius have both been affected. It is hoped that she will recover the use of her neck muscles.

3. The Province of Ha Tay

In 1964 the provinces of Ha Dong and Son Tay amalgamated to form the single province of Ha Tay. This new province has eighteen districts and two former provincial capitals, both now destroyed. Ha Tay has a population of about 1,400,000. The province is made up of three distinct regions: mountains and forests, semi-mountainous areas, and flat delta-land. Although agriculture is a principal source of wealth, handicrafts are an important factor too, accounting for 30 per cent of total output. The province produces an average of 1.7 tons of rice per acre. It is making every effort to develop dry crops such as sweet potato and maize, pig-breeding, and industrial plants, including jute. It has suffered fewer raids than the national average. According to official figures, the Ha Tay militia had brought down forty-seven aircraft in the period ending 14 October 1967.

The Commune of Hoa Xa

Vu Van Tuoc of the Party's District Committee:

The commune of Hoa Xa has two co-operatives: a handicrafts co-operative employing a thousand people and a farming co-operative employing about 500. The total population is in the region of 4,500. Seventy per cent of the inhabitants make their living from handicrafts. These take various forms, but since the American attacks started we have been instructed to concentrate our efforts on weaving clothing materials and mosquito nets.

All the women at our spinning mill are armed with rifles, and the workshops are surrounded by a whole system of dugouts and shelters. Along the embankment we have several platoons of militiawomen armed with 12 x 7 machine-guns. Our buildings are visible, and I think we shall be bombed before long.

In this area, weaving dates back several centuries to the days of the Les[1]. Under the French, it was just possible to make a living out of weaving; but hundreds of workers had to go and look for work elsewhere. Since the revolution, the Party has helped us to reorganize completely and today we are semi-mechanized. We have looms with 105 spindles. In the old days, working methods were crude and the spindles had to be operated with the feet, whereas today the worker can stand and control every function of the machine with lengthwise movements of the arm. This has increased our output a hundredfold. After 1955 the state supplied us with wood and iron so that we could raise the quantity and quality of our machines. In 1966 we were helped and advised by three Grade 2 technical cadres from Hanoi, and in 1960 we had the services of an engineer – a woman who had been trained abroad.

1. The most illustrious dynasty in the history of Vietnam (fifteenth to seventeenth century).

In 1957 we borrowed 50,000 dongs from the state, a debt which we cleared in 1963. At that time (1956–9) we had not yet formed ourselves into a co-operative. The activities of the various working groups were controlled by a committee of fifteen.

Late in 1959 and early in 1960 we succeeded in organizing eight co-operatives, the largest consisting of 150 members and the smallest of fifty. These were rudimentary co-operatives; but in October 1960, after a period of research and examination, we welded them into a single advanced co-operative. Between August and October we had the workers form themselves into a number of study groups, so that they could draw up proposals concerning the nature of the advanced co-operative. What should be preserved? Should equipment remain in private hands or should it be pooled? In the end, we all decided in favour of collectivization. It was a long campaign, lasting two months, and applications for membership began to pour in. We were convinced that an advanced co-operative would enable us to achieve higher productivity. All the same, there were some workers who did not want to join. Thirty-three of them delayed doing so until April 1961. Subsequently, when they saw it was to their own good, they put in their applications. In the first place, membership brought political advantages: those who had been willing to join were regarded as trendsetters, and were generally looked up to. (Their children made fun of those whose parents had not become members.) In the second place, it brought financial advantages. If a member fell ill, he was entitled to a hospital bed and the co-operative paid him 0.80 dongs a day. When a woman member had a baby, she received a bonus of a month's pay – say fifteen dongs – plus two dongs for every month of membership after the first year. In the case of co-operators with a child attending nursery school, the family paid 0.60 dongs a month and the co-operative added 0.80 dongs. If there were two children at nursery school, the co-operator paid one dong and the co-operative 0.50. If there were three, the co-operator paid 1.20 dongs and the co-operative 1.80. As regards older children, large families were subsidized by the co-operative, receiving between 5 and 30 per cent of school fees. Families with more than four children are entitled to a subsidy of over 9 per cent. As for the children of co-operators who are away on military service, their education is subsidized by up to 30 per cent. In some cases – as, for instance, when a co-operator falls sick or has an accident at work – benefits ranging from 5 to 50 per cent (and occasionally even 100 per cent) of the normal wage are paid over a period of several months. Lastly – and lastly is the right word! – there is another advantage: when a co-operator or a member of his family dies, the co-operative provides a coffin free of charge. The official price of a coffin is forty dongs, plus one dong for a bundle of joss-sticks, so this represents a saving of forty-one dongs. On the free market, by the way, a coffin fetches over 100 dongs!

In the early days of the co-operative there was a decline in results because of the mismanagement of a very large sum of invested capital. In 1961, the average income per head, including members' families, was only ten dongs. In 1962 we made headway, and the figure rose to 13.40 dongs. In 1963 it was 14.10 dongs, in 64 14.70 dongs, and in 65 15.10 dongs. In 66 it rose to over seventeen dongs. Dissatisfied members were told that difficulties were only to be expected; that the present bad patch was due to the faulty handling of money; that working independently certainly had its advantages, for when a man worked solely for himself he was free to spend as much as he could earn; that there was no depreciation involved; and that although comparisons tended to show that private work was more profitable, it was only fair to consider the size of the capital investment and the difficulties involved in administering it – consider the problems of managing even a small household. We acknowledged our deficiencies and the blunders made by our officials, who had no experience of collective management; we also drew attention to the fact that output had not been high enough. In those days there were far fewer co-operators than there are now, and some families were seriously thinking of leaving the co-operative and working for themselves again. So we launched two political campaigns, one to explain our policies and the other to rekindle memories of the past. We recalled the poverty and oppression of feudal times, the conditions which had existed under the French, and how hard it had been to survive in those days. In comparison, the Party had worked wonders; and if it had now decided to proceed to collectivization, that – we said – was for the purpose of bringing about a general improvement. After two months of propaganda and discussion, the eighteen households which had been anxious to leave the co-operative agreed to stay. And no one else left. So then we set up another series of study groups with the aim of improving production and management; the idea was that every worker should try to find the roots of our troubles. And we arrived at the following conclusion: *all co-operators must be free to deliberate democratically about how production is to be organized. The co-operators must participate in the management of labour and of the tools of work. That is essential.* We also encouraged a competitive approach to work, based on patriotism, and at the same time we provided material rewards for good workers: five extra dongs for an individual good worker at the end of a six-month period, or thirty to fifty dongs for a good gang. In this way we supplied a combination of moral and material inducements . . .

In 1960 we had 5,000 dongs. Today our account stands at 100,000. The machinery is valued at 250,000 dongs, and the buildings at 100,000; all loans for these items have been repaid. In 1960 the average worker's wage was about twenty-five dongs a month; it has now risen to about forty. Our co-operative returns some of the best production figures in the country, and our rates of pay are correspondingly high. In 1966 we were 25 per cent above the norm.

A Handicrafts Co-operative

There are about 1,000 full-time and 500 part-time workers.

The Workers' Assembly elects a twenty-one-member Management Committee, which holds office for a year. The Management Committee in turn elects a standing committee of seven, picked from its own ranks. There is a chairman, who has overall control of the co-operative, and four vice-chairmen who are responsible for planning, finance, technical problems and supplies respectively. The sixth member is in charge of social and cultural affairs, and the seventh manages an experimental workshop which exists for the purpose of increasing output and improving general organization.

Each of the other fourteen members of the Management Committee serves as manager of a workshop; it is their job to see that every link in the chain of production functions correctly and produces the best possible results. The Management Committee meets every month to examine progress. The Workers' General Assembly convenes once a quarter and discusses general developments in production. Subject to a two-thirds majority of its own members, the Assembly is empowered to dismiss any member of the Management Committee. This system has been in operation since 1960. Of the twenty-one members of the Management Committee of this particular co-operative, fourteen are Party members and seven belong to the Young Workers[2].

The Supervisory Committee is made up of nine members, elected by secret ballot, and has full authority to look into the affairs of the Management Committee. The head of the

2. There are eighty Party members in the commune as a whole; another twenty are absent on army service. In the co-operative there are thirty-eight out of a previous total of fifty-four.

Supervisory Committee is a Party member and he is also deputy head of the local security service. The Supervisory Committee has three full-time members; the other six supervise the work of the production groups. Like the Management Committee, it holds office for a year, and its officers are subject to dismissal by a two-thirds majority of the General Assembly. One member was dismissed in 1964, on grounds of maladministration. Any co-operator is free to put up as a candidate or be nominated by his comrades. In 1966 there were thirty-three candidates for the Management Committee and fifteen for the Supervisory Committee.

The basic unit within the co-operative is the section, comprising six to eight workers. Next comes the gang, made up of three sections. Each section elects its own chief and deputy chief. There are five gangs to a workshop. Each of the eight workshops in the co-operative is run by a member of the Management Committee; and in every workshop there is a cell made up of five to eight members, who rank as assistant heads of workshop.

Women hold 40 per cent of the positions of responsibility within the co-operative, and 30 per cent of those within the Party. They form 70 per cent of the staff. There is a special mutual-aid organization to cope with the needs arising from childbirth.

The workshops also have their own militia groups, operating in squads of ten and platoons of thirty. There are two distinct categories. The first consists of co-operators who will soon be leaving the commune to join the army; they continue to produce goods, but are also receiving a daily course in weapon training. The other category is responsible for local defence; these are elderly men or specially trained young girls armed with 12 x 7s or 37 mm. Finally, all workers keep a rifle hanging beside their looms.

Wages are directly related to the task performed. For instance, a bundle of 4.5 thread will produce fifty-two yards of cloth. The task will keep two co-operators busy for fourteen hours, and the rate for the job is ten dongs. These ten dongs do not include the 15 per cent of the total sum which the co-operative retains as accumulated capital or the 32 per cent which it deducts to cover the cost of raw materials. The ten dongs are divided up as follows: weaving and folding, 66 per cent; sundry other operations (washing, drying, winding-on, etc.), 34 per cent. The technicians' wages are higher – seventy-two dongs a month. There are two of them. On average, the workers earn forty dongs. The chairman of the Management Committee used to get seventy-five dongs, but has taken a cut of twenty-five since escalation began, as a contribution to the war effort.

The machines operate non-stop, except from 11 p.m. till 4 a.m. The rest of the time, the families work in shifts. The co-operators put in a seventy- or even eighty-hour week. Most households earn between eighty and ninety dongs. As regards productivity: two workers manufacture fifty-five yards of mosquito-netting every eight hours.

A Bombed Village

Kim Bai in the district of Thanh Oai

At 12.45 p.m. on 26 October 1967 several American F 105s appeared over Kim Bai, the main community centre in the district of Thanh Oai. One wave of aircraft approached from the south-west, the other from the north-west. The village lies along Route Provinciale No. 22 (Hanoi–Hoa Binh). The planes dived down over the central hamlet and dropped their bombs. Seventeen people were killed, including five women and three children. There were twenty-two other casualties – ten of them women. The hamlet had 300 inhabitants. Material damage was extensive. Among the buildings destroyed were a children's nursery, a dispensary, a restaurant, a rice ware-house, five workshops manufacturing furniture and farm tools, and the post office. Twenty-nine houses were badly battered. All of these were solidly constructed buildings, erected since 1960. I drove to this village on 29 October.

Nguyen Thi Xuan, peasant, aged thirty:

My cousin got killed in the raid. Her name was Nguyen Thi Nga; she was twenty-seven. It happened three days ago, round about noon. I heard an explosion and saw flames. Two of the houses close to mine caught fire, and I hurried along the street to help put out the blaze. Other people came to the rescue, too. I saw two women lying in the roadway, seriously wounded. I called out to them, but they didn't answer. I shouted for assistance. People came, carrying door-leaves in lieu of stretchers, and took them as far as the dam, where some lorries were waiting. They were driven to hospital. I let the other women accompany the wounded and went back to see if there were any others in or near the dugouts. . . . The two women reached hospital at about one o'clock and were given proper treatment.

One of them died at three in the afternoon, the other at four. The first had been wounded all over; the second had received bad injuries to her head and stomach, and was riddled with shrapnel. One was twenty-four. Her name was Chu Thi Thoan. She had one child and was expecting another in six months' time. The other woman was my cousin Nguyen Thi Nga. She was twenty-seven and had two children aged six and four. When I returned to the scene, I saw ten or a dozen other wounded. Most of the people who got killed were lying in the open street.

They came in two waves. The first wave kept up the attack for ten minutes. The second wave appeared a quarter of an hour later and stayed for fifteen minutes. The planes belonging to the first wave bombed the road, and those belonging to the second bombed the village. After the explosions, the whole village was covered in smoke. The hamlet was hit by an onrush of smoke and dust that brought several houses crashing down. The water in the ponds was pitch black, and so were the clothes hanging from the lines. Bits of roofing were strewn all over the place. We knew the American planes might come and bomb us, and that is why we dug trenches.

There are no military objectives here, but they have destroyed every modern building we owned.

Chu Thi Mao, peasant, aged thirty-nine:

I am the aunt of Chu Thi Thoan, who got killed. She was twenty-four. Her husband refuses to see anyone, and her father here doesn't feel like talking.

Round about midday she and two other women were coming back from the paddy-fields, where they had been growing azolla. The other two were lucky, but Thoan got killed by flying shrapnel. It was my husband – the girl's uncle – who saw what happened and told me about it. He went out into the square and saw his niece lying in a pool of blood. She called out to him. 'Uncle,' she said, 'I'm dying.' Then he saw she was wounded in the back. He and another member of the militia brought a stretcher and carried her to safety. The orderlies came. They gave her an emergency dressing and moved her to a point near the dam. A lorry came and took her and some of the other wounded to hospital. Relatives sobbed and screamed and tried to board the lorry in an attempt to travel with them, but they were stopped from doing so. The casualties were placed in the care of a nurse, a member of the militia and two women from the Combatants' Welfare Association. On the way to hospital she called out the names of her husband and her sixteen-month-old daughter. She died at the end of the journey. The news reached us at about two o'clock. A member of the hospital staff came out and asked if there were any members of her family present, as her clothes needed to be changed. She had no kin with her, so the militiaman helped the hospital workers to remove her torn clothing and wrap her in a sheet. They lost no time in reporting her death to the village, and her body was back here by seven o'clock.

The dead woman's father said: 'I feel full of hatred towards the American aggressors. We were working our land, that's all; what did they come and kill us for?'

Nguyen Thi Mui, peasant, aged thirty-four:

I was on my way back from the paddy-fields. I was just setting my bundles of rice down in the depot yard when I heard the roar of exploding bombs. My husband was still out on the road. I ran and took cover in a school shelter about a hundred yards away. I was crouching there, with a few other women from the co-operative, when someone came and told us that the planes had bombed the further hamlet, which was where my husband was. I told the women he had been killed for sure. 'No, no,' they said, 'he will have taken shelter. You can bet your life he didn't hang about waiting for the bombs to fall.' But I just knew, in my heart, that my husband was dead.

As soon as the planes had gone I hurried back, crying as I ran. The territorials and wardens were already clearing debris from the spot close to the inn where my husband had been killed. There were dead bodies lying about. I was stopped and advised to go home. The planes might come back, they said, and it was dangerous to hang about. I was desperate to see my husband, but they wouldn't let me stay. A member of the militia took me to a house and made sure I stayed there. Half an hour later I was allowed to go and see my husband, who had been moved over two hundred yards from where the bomb had fallen. They let me look at the coffin. They lifted the lid only slightly, so that I could see my husband's face, but I saw blood-red bandages round his stomach. A whole row of people prevented me from looking any longer, because I am pregnant. I stayed there, though. I sat beside the closed coffin until eight in the evening. I had my eldest daughter with me. The three younger children were kept away until the funeral, when they were allowed to accompany their father to the cemetery.

We farm our land. That's all we do, farm our land. And suddenly they come here and kill us. I don't know what to say.

The worst casualties were transferred to the provincial hospital; the rest were dealt with at district or commune level. After receiving preliminary treatment at the district hospital, the three most serious cases were moved to the provincial hospital during the late afternoon of 26 October. The head surgeon there, Hoang Tach To, is a graduate of the Faculty of Medicine in Paris.

The two survivors were resting at the time of my visit. On arrival, they had been given a blood transfusion and dry plasma. The operations were carried out next day. One of them had a perforating wound in the right leg – a vascular injury. A section of the right heel has now been amputated. The wound was cleansed, the bone scraped, the marrow reconstituted. The other survivor – Tran Van Kim, a seventeen-year-old blacksmith – had a large wound in the right shoulder, with muscular damage and profuse bleeding. The wound was cleansed, the flow of bleeding stopped and the muscle stitched.

The condition of both these casualties was now regarded as satisfactory. But a third victim, with wounds to the face and abdomen, died after two whole days on the operating table.

A Nursery School

Hoa Xa commune in the district of Hung Hoa

I paid a visit to the nursery school. The building is modern and built to last. The girl in charge is a slender, pretty girl named Nguyen Thi Hoa; she is twenty-one. She has fifty-three children in her care, all aged between three and six. They greeted us with a little song. There is a long line of towels, individually embroidered with the children's names. Toys hang from the wall: a mobile consisting of green fish made from woven leaves; paper cutouts; items of needlework; seashells strung together in arresting shapes and patterns. There are six classes like this within the commune. The busiest has sixty children, the slackest thirty; the average is about forty. Each production group has its own nursery school. Parents pay 0.60 dongs a month to cover expenses. The co-operative adds 0.40 dongs. The child-minders are paid a maximum of forty-five dongs and a minimum of forty. In the case of a nursery school attached to a farming co-operative, the child-minder is remunerated in points – i.e. rice. But where the school is attached to a handicrafts co-operative, she is paid in hard cash. The nursery is open from six till eleven and two till 5.30. Meals are taken at home. On arrival in the mornings, the children do exercises for fifteen minutes and are then checked for cleanliness. They are taught to take care of their own clothes and belongings. Next comes a recreation period of twenty minutes; afterwards they are told a story; then they play. I asked Nguyen Thi Hoa to tell us a story. All the children sat down while she prepared a miniature stage which was hidden behind a curtain. She drew on a pair of glove-puppets and said: 'Now, fold your arms, children. I'm going to tell you a story. It's the one about the little pig who wanted to make friends.' She was silent for a moment, then she continued: 'A little rabbit has just been whispering in my ear. He says, please can *he* tell the story instead of me? What do you think, children? Shall we let him?' 'Yes! Yes!' cried the children. 'All right, but you must be quiet so that you will be sure of hearing him . . .' Whereupon the little rabbit appeared. 'Hullo, playmates,' he said, 'I *am* glad to see you, and I hope you are going to enjoy my story. I've come all the way from the forest especially to tell it to you.' A complete hush came over the children. And this is the story the rabbit told: 'I was out flower-picking in a big forest where there were lots of trees and plants when who should I meet but a little pig. "Come over here, little pig," I called. And he came bounding towards me. I was ever so glad to see the little pig bounding towards me, but when he reached me I wasn't glad at all. He was very, very dirty, and I just didn't want him as a playmate. "Oh, no," I said, "you're far too dirty. You must go and have a wash. Then, when you come back, we'll have a nice game." "But I dare not have a wash," said the little pig. "The water is too cold." And he wandered away, all on his own. He searched the forest, looking for friends, but he couldn't find any. He walked and walked until at last he found a little deer. "Come here, little deer," he said, "come and play with me." And he went over to him. But the little deer wouldn't have anything to do with him either. Like me, he thought the little pig was too dirty. "You'll have to play by yourself," he said. So the little pig went on his way again. He felt ever so sad. "That makes two animals I've met," he said. "One was a rabbit and one was a deer, and neither would play with me." After a while he met the wolf. "Oh, I'm so glad to see you!" he said. "Do come and play with me." But the wolf gave the same answer as the others. He advised the little pig to go and take a bath in the river. Once again the little pig said: "No, it's too cold." And so he walked on and on, all by himself, until evening came. Then he came to a beautiful lake, and on the lake he saw a swan, and the little pig called out to him. "Oh, swan, swan! Come on, swan! Come and play with me!" The swan looked up, and when he saw the little pig he shouted "Quack-quack-quack-quack-quack!" This was to show how glad he was, for he had been feeling very lonely too. "Come and play with me, little pig," he said, "come and have a bath!" The little pig came nearer and nearer until he was standing right beside the lake. And then he saw how dirty his face was, and all the rest of him too, and he realized why other people hadn't wanted to play with him. "All right," he said, "I'll play with you, I'll have a bath." And with that the little pig jumped into the water. The swan swam over and helped him, splashing water over his head and washing all the dirt off. And the little pig grew cleaner and cleaner until his skin shone pink. And he realized how nice it was to be clean, and saw that this was the right way to set about making friends. Afterwards, he and the swan went off in search of the other three – the wolf, the deer and the rabbit – and for days and days and days the five of them rambled about the country-side, playing happily together. It's the same with you children: if you want to make friends, you must never forget to wash yourselves each day; then you will be nice to look at.'

The story was over. The rabbit did a special dance for his audience. Nguyen Thi Hoa sang them a song, a very pretty song. Then she said: 'Now children, where do you run to when you see or hear an aeroplane?' And the children replied: 'To the trenches.' And the girl continued: 'Recently I visited a school which had been bombed by aeroplanes, and now I'm going to tell you another story. . . . One day the sun was shining bright, and at Miss Thuy's nursery school everything was peaceful and merry. The children were having lots of fun. Suddenly the planes came. "Everyone into the trenches," said Miss Thuy to the children. And the children ran as fast as they could, for the aeroplanes began to swoop on Miss Thuy's school like a swarm of black crows. But nearly all the children were safe inside the trenches, with their straw-plaited helmets on their heads and their Red Cross kits slung over their shoulders. Three bombs went off – Bang! Bang! Bang! – and the children covered their ears with their hands and huddled against one another. Miss Thuy told them to keep quite still. When the raid was over, Miss Thuy made the rounds of the two trenches. Alas, there were two children who had not taken cover in time. They hadn't been quick enough, and the shrapnel had caught them. They were seriously wounded and had to be taken to the district hospital.

'There!' said Nguyen Thi Hoa. 'There were two victims. Two of your little comrades were wounded. And why? Because they didn't get into the trench in time. They got hurt by the American planes. So what must you always do, children?'

'Get into the trench,' they replied.

'That's right,' she told them. 'And another thing: you must always come straight to school. You must never loiter on the way, for if we are to fight the Americans your father needs to be in the army, your mother needs to be in the fields, and you need to be at school. And if ever you hear the sound of planes, you must all get into the trenches. Because American planes are very cruel. They have wounded your little friends, and you must never forget to have your straw-plaited helmets and your Red Cross kits with you.'

At this point, all the children began to sing a song about the wickedness of aircraft, the ugly roar and whine they made, and how children must hurry to the shelters whenever they attacked.

'The best way for you to resist the Americans,' Nguyen Thi Hoa said in conclusion, 'is to study harder. Some members of your families fight. Others produce our food and the other things we need. You must study hard.'

Personal Statements

Phung Thi Bach Tuyet, peasant, aged twenty, unmarried. Inside her cob-walled house are a table, two benches, and a pair of beds fitted with mosquito nets:

I come from a family of landless peasants. Under the land reform programme we received 1.2 maus. I have six brothers and sisters. My two elder sisters are married, and my elder brother is in the army. So is my younger brother. My other two sisters are both members of the co-operative. I haven't had any news of my brothers. My elder sisters have been educated to Class 7 standard, and the two younger girls are in Classes 4 and 5. My young brother has completed seven classes, and my older brother nine. In 1955 I hadn't yet been to school, though I was eight, and when the land reform scheme was introduced I was given extra coaching. In this way I completed six classes after the revolution. I am still carrying on with my studies. My eldest sister is a textile worker; the other one is at the knitting factory. I joined the co-operative in 1959, and since 1962 I have been second-in-command of the local militia. I have played my part in production and, since the aggression began, in military training. At the end of 1964 I was sent to the provincial capital to study nursing. The course lasted nine months.

As soon as I returned to the village I was put in charge of a heavy-machine-gun team. We and the rest of the platoon were given a special training course by a regular army officer. The officer spent five days with us, but we trained on our own for a whole month, getting plenty of practice at stripping the gun and reassembling it.

We use mobile guns because it is very dangerous to remain in any one spot for long. In view of our morale and experience, though, I'm sure the US Air Force will never succeed in knocking us out. It takes us only ten minutes to move to another position and continue the fight from there. The girls in my platoon are all between the ages of seventeen and twenty. Some have been educated to Class 5 standard, others to Class 7. There are sixteen of us, and a party of four or six – plus an observer – remains on duty round the clock. We operate a roster system, so that all of us can contribute to production. I am paid by the co-operative, and I receive fifteen points a day when I am on guard.

On 19 August 1967 we saw an American plane flying home after bombing another area. It flew over our commune without diving, but we opened fire and it came down in flames. The pilot was killed. The plane had been flying at about 3,000 feet; it's very hard to hit one flying higher than 3,000. If it dives, you shoot straight at it. We hit this one sideways on. It was the girls who brought it down. The platoon was very pleased.

At present we are waiting to receive some 37 mm. guns – a very effective anti-aircraft weapon. The elderly men, who have a platoon of their own, are equipped with two 12 x 7 machine-guns and will soon be getting a third. But it is the girls who will have the use of the 37 mms. The old men are keen enough: it took them only three days' training to grasp the main points. But there's no getting away from it: they don't measure up to us. Their sight is deteriorating, and they aren't very agile. Only 70 per cent of them have satisfied all the required standards, whereas every one of the girls has passed with flying colours. The old women back at the village have set up a Combatants' Welfare Association, and every month they visit us and bring us presents: tea, bananas, sweets, beer, towels. . . . Within fifteen minutes of our shooting down the plane, they all trooped out to see us and we had quite a party. All of us subscribe to the 'Five Wells' and the 'Three Tasks'. The 'Five Wells' are: to produce well; to fight well; to economize well; to carry out directives well; and to bring up our children well. The 'Three Tasks' are: to fight and produce well; to take over the jobs of husbands and other young men so that they may join the army; and to mobilize husbands and other young men so that they may fulfil their tasks at the front. Many men have gone away in the past two years. Previously women were regarded as mere housewives, but now all that has changed. The man does the housework without waiting for the woman, just as the woman used to do it without waiting for the man. In the old days the man took all the decisions and would then pass them on to his wife in his own good time. He wouldn't dare do that any more: he is careful to consult his wife about everything. At one time, women who had a lot of children were in no position to participate in anything, not even during the early years of the revolution. Today women have organized their lives so that they are not so busy. They are able to play a full part in social affairs, even if they have seven children. They can even join the militia, for their children go to school; the really young ones spend most of the day at the nursery, where they are well looked after. Women occupy nearly 60 per cent of the posts in the local People's Councils, and the vice-chairman of the Administrative Committee is a woman. We also have a woman working as a qualified medical auxiliary. Nearly all our nurses are women. There is a woman vice-chairman in the handicrafts co-operative, and a good many women are on the Management Committee and Supervisory Committee. All this derives from the Party's willingness to give thought to such matters and educate the masses. To an even greater degree, it stems from the strong convictions of women themselves: they woke up to the fact that they were capable of doing the same jobs as men, and that they ought therefore to be placed on an equal footing. The military service we have performed since the attacks started has greatly furthered our cause. The local army chief is a woman, and so is the deputy political commissar.

Nguyen Thi Hue, peasant, aged forty-five. She lives in a cob-walled house with two beds and a stool:

I was born into a family of landless peasants. My mother died when I was seven, and my father when I was twelve. My parents died in the province of Hung Yen. I entered the service of a mandarin landowner. He was the district ruler. As I was an orphan, he more or less adopted me. A foster-daughter was expected to do all kinds of jobs, and she received no pay for her work. The mandarin died, and his wife then adopted me. She had one house in Hanoi and another at Lac Dao, in the province of Hung Yen; so sometimes we lived in Lac Dao and sometimes in Hanoi.

I had to do the housework, but I wasn't treated badly. She behaved as if I really were her daughter, so I went on working for her year after year. On my wedding day she gave us a month's supply of rice, about seventy pounds. My husband came to live with me in my foster-mother's house, for I continued to do the chores for her. My husband worked as a labourer for other landowners. He didn't work for my foster-mother, for by then she had sold her acres and gone into business. Things changed soon after I married. The French troops moved into the area and my foster-mother went to Hanoi, leaving me to look after the house. We didn't make any money from the fruit and vegetables in her allotment, for once a month she came out and sold them. My husband often had to hide, for there was an army post less than a quarter of a mile away and he was young enough to have to do forced labour. So he went away and tried to get work at a safe distance, while I rented five saos from a landowner. I worked these five saos all on my own. They brought me in four hundredweights of rice a year, and I had to give half to the man who owned the land. My husband could only help occasionally, for the paddy-fields were dangerously close to the army post. Every so often I used to go to Hanoi and buy salt, which I would afterwards sell in Lac Dao. After three years, we had a daughter. My husband was still hiding, to avoid being conscripted into the puppet army; so I had to do his share of forced labour. I used to go to the post once a week, with a party of old women. If it hadn't been for the old women, I should have been raped by the Moroccans – Thabors they were called. One day there were only a few old women at the post and the French were out on a mopping-up operation. The Moroccans who had stayed behind grabbed me and tried to rape me. I shouted my head off, and my screams roused the Vietnamese political prisoners who were working in the post; they came rushing to the rescue and I managed to make my escape. I left the village at once, and so did my husband. Luckily my children were already in Hanoi: my daughter was over a year old by then. We didn't work for my foster-mother in Hanoi. We rented a house on the outskirts of town, and my husband plied for hire with a cycle-rickshaw. Two years later we had another son: he's twelve now. We earned enough to keep us going. I used to sell vegetables. In 1955 we came back to the village. This one, I mean – my husband's father's village. We moved in with my husband's uncle. We received a provisional grant of a mau under the land reform programme. We were a family of five at the time, and we produced more rice than we required for our own needs. In that first year – 1955 – we had a surplus of two hundred-weights. We also reared one or two pigs a year, and in 1956 our rice surplus was nearly four hundredweights. In 56 we were given another plot of land: I can't remember how big it was, but it was more than we had before. Altogether we had about two maus, and we were classified as poor peasants. We had our fourth son, who is now eight. At about that time we set up mutual-aid teams and found that by exchanging labour we could produce more. After the co-operative began, we received a maximum of four and a minimum of two hundredweights of surplus rice a year. The co-operative brought a number of advantages. There was a guaranteed working week, even in slack periods of the year, so that we could always count on getting enough rice to live on. The children were able to go to school: three of mine were attending lessons then. I was pregnant during the harvest season, so I was given a month off and granted a free allocation of rice – forty-five pounds in all. I didn't have to pay anything towards the maternity costs. Also, we women are entitled to attend meetings and have our proper say.

I've been really lucky. My husband was very easy to get on with: we never quarrelled. Another thing, I didn't have to knuckle under to any in-laws. Some couples used to quarrel all the time, and there were husbands who used to beat their wives. Even in our own case, my husband's voice used to carry more weight than mine before the revolution – whereas after-wards we decided everything between us. In the old days women had no social standing, no authority: they were just there to do the housework and toil in the fields. But today women hold official posts and are heads of production groups. We are free to criticize the efforts of those in authority – a thing we were never allowed to do in the past; why, we weren't even permitted to speak in the presence of the elders! Now we can go to meetings and voice as many criticisms as we like. Life was good until my husband got killed. The day it happened, we went to market. I wanted to buy some material from the State Store, and my husband wanted to buy a piglet. He left home at about eight in the morning, half an hour ahead of me. When I got to the market-place, I saw my husband haggling over the price of the piglet. I left him there and went to the store. I had just handed over fifteen dongs for my length of material when someone rushed in from the cycle market and shouted: 'The planes are coming!' We all hurried out of the store. I didn't even have time to collect my change. We pushed and shoved a bit in our haste to get clear of the building. Then we scattered. I started running towards the bridge. As I reached it I heard the roar of planes and saw four of them approaching. Two were flying fairly high, but the other two were much lower. I saw the two lower ones release their bombs, and I flung myself down beside a pile of stones. I heard the bombs explode. Those which burst in the water were fairly quiet, but the bombs which landed at the foot of the dam made a terrible noise. The bomb lying quite close to my husband's body had not gone off, but he had been hit by shrapnel from another. His body looked quite unharmed when I found it. There was no sign of a wound. He lay there as though he were asleep, without a mark on his clothes; his hat was missing, that was all. But he was surrounded by eight or nine other bodies, and when I saw him lying among them I realized that the worst had happened and that there was no possibility of his coming back to life. I stayed there for an hour, crying helplessly, and then some people from the co-operative came and took the bodies away. The co-operative gave me a coffin and two yards of mosquito-netting to wrap the body in.

My two eldest children were growing up fast by then, and they were able to step into my husband's shoes as full-time workers; so we didn't go short of food. We didn't achieve a surplus, though – just enough to keep us going. Last year we were hard up for rice during the lean season, and the co-operative gave us thirty-three pounds of rice for the children. The youngest is now old enough to go to school. The eldest boy and girl are seventeen and fifteen. They've left school. One of them has reached Class 5 standard, the other Class 4; they are pulling their weight in production. We have half a sao for growing vegetables, and on average we sell more than a hundred dongs' worth a year. A few months ago I sold a ninety-pound pig for sixty dongs, and we have also earned a bit extra by minding the co-operative's buffalo. We have enough to live on, but there is no chance of our buying any furniture. This house was built by my husband, a year before he died. Now I am all alone. My seventeen-year-old son is almost old enough to join the army, and when he does I shan't have anyone to lean on. I keep telling him his rightful place is here, but he is determined to join up and avenge his father's death. I don't want him to go, but I feel certain he will. He has already volunteered twice. They turned him down because he was too short and underweight. But I can sense that he will be leaving soon, and it is very hard for me to have to rear my children all on my own.

Do Hong, peasant, aged thirty-nine, born in the village of Hoa Xa. He lives in a permanently built house with a thatch roof. There are two beds, both hung with mosquito nets, and two stools. Seven diplomas are displayed on the walls. He owns a bicycle:

My mother died when I was eight. She was a villager, whereas my father and my sister and I used to live in Hanoi. He was a coolie, a road-sweeper. A year after my mother died he remarried, and we children couldn't get on with his second wife. My sister went into service, while I wandered from place to place, playing cards and marbles for money. Eventually a tailor took me in and gave me board and lodging; but soon afterwards he lost all he owned in a card game and I had to come back to my native village. I was ten years old at the time. Some of my family were still living in the village, and I was given the job of minding my uncle's buffalo. My uncle's family owned two and a half maus of land and earned a living by peddling rice. Up to the age of nineteen I shared in every kind of work: ploughing, minding the ox, weeding, spreading manure. . . . My uncle kept me in food and clothes but did not pay me a wage. My uncle gave me a hard time, but his wife was even worse. She used to hurl abuse at me. 'You don't produce enough,' she would say. 'You spend more time eating than working.'

In 1950 the French moved in and started building posts. There was one a quarter of a mile away, manned by French and puppet troops. I've forgotten how many there were of them. I had learned to weave when I was seventeen – it was a common skill here in the village – and after the French came I moved to Thanh Hoa and worked for a peasant who owned a loom. I got married at twenty. My wife was from the same village, and we married in Thanh Hoa. She used to help me with the winding and spinning, and this made us self-supporting. With the return of peace in 1954, we were both repatriated to our own village. We moved in with my sister-in-law and her family: that was in the days before we had children. We received a temporary grant of one mau under the land reform scheme. At the end of 1954 my wife gave birth to a daughter. In 1956 we were classified as poor peasants and told to keep the mau we had been given; we weren't allotted any extra land, but my family was awarded a fourth share in a buffalo. Early in 1957 we built a three-room cottage, and at the end of the year my wife gave birth to a son. Life became steadily more comfortable after we received that grant of land. On average we managed to put by six hundredweights of rice a year and sell over two hundredweights of pig. In addition to all this, we were making rather more than a hundred dongs a year from the sale of home-grown vegetables.

When the land reform programme was introduced, there were reckoned to be six landowners in the neighbourhood. The biggest was a man called Ninh. He owned the largest house in the village. He was a mandarin and had been a district ruler. Today his house serves as the Party's reception centre, and also as the museum. He owned fifty maus, eight of which were used for growing longans.

In 1954 he fled to the south, together with all the other landowners. During the whole of the land reform programme, there was only one case in which an error was committed. Nhuan was suspected of and charged with being a landowner. He had six maus. His wife and children were among those who brought the charge, and he admitted it. A whole year went by before this mistake was put right. In the meantime all his lands were taken from him, and his house as well. He was left with only one room, which he had to share with the wife and children who had accused him. The substance of the charge was that he owned more paddy-fields than he could cultivate; and because he hired labourers to help him he was regarded as having exploited the peasants. He was indicted before the assembled villagers and immediately admitted that he was a landowner. He was also accused of being a member of the Council of Notables and harbouring reactionaries in his house. When the mistake was put right, it was acknowledged that he had quite a large family: there were seven mouths to be fed. As a result, he was reclassified as a 'well-off peasant'. Two maus were returned to him for cultivation, while the state bought the other six. He was given some money, and his house was handed back to him. He himself admitted that it was only right and proper that he should sell these six maus to the state, since it was irregular for a peasant to own more paddy-fields than he could cultivate. He and his wife and children continued to live on good terms. He was rehabilitated. The news was announced at a special meeting attended by all the villagers. It came as a bombshell. The so-called landowner had not protested, and yet suddenly a group of Party officials arrived in the commune and declared that an error had been committed, an error that must be put right.

Meanwhile my own family had become quite well-off. We gave up weaving and spent all our time on the land. I was one of the first to volunteer for membership of the co-operative in 1958. We were told what a co-operative was, and how it would work. It sounded a good scheme to me: if a man fell sick, he could count on receiving assistance. Before the co-operative was set up, we tried a system of mutual aid. Twenty-seven households in the hamlet formed themselves into teams which could help out wherever they were needed. All the families were agreed that the scheme offered a good many advantages. In the first place, some peasants were short of tools and oxen and obviously benefited from a pooling system. In the second place, we were able to get on faster at harvest time and other key moments in the year, and so we were in a position to produce more. This mutual-aid venture lasted a year, spanning 1957. I produced four hundredweights more rice that year than in the previous year. Early in 1958 I joined the co-operative. At that stage it was only a small-scale co-operative, made up of twenty-seven households. It was fairly easy to run: we didn't encounter any major difficulties, and we were already used to working together. That year I managed to put by fourteen hundredweights of rice. Our takings were good for a family of five. There were two full-time workers in the household: my wife and myself. In 1961 the big co-operative was set up, covering the whole commune. It took a long time because there were some peasants who did not want to join at all, or who thought it was better to continue with the mutual-aid scheme than to form a large co-operative. Early in 1961 one of the heads of the Party's Central Committee – I forget his name – came to the village and explained the advantages which a co-operative would bring. Everyone agreed to join for a trial period. In that first year my family achieved a surplus of sixteen hundredweights. At the beginning of 1962 my wife gave birth to another child – a girl. In 1962 we achieved a similar surplus, almost sixteen hundredweights. In 1963 our surplus rose to a ton, and halfway through the year we had this house built: it took a month and cost us 900 dongs. The benefits of forming a co-operative became obvious to us straight away: in 1961 we installed a diesel pump, and the new drainage system made it possible for us to fight drought.

The abolition of privately owned plots meant that the paddy-fields became generally larger. As a result, ploughing took far less time and productivity was nearly doubled. The only people to whom the co-operative brought hardship were those who could not provide much full-time, able-bodied labour: they had no hope of achieving a large number of points. And they were wholly dependent on the points they earned in the fields, whereas in the past they had been able to do other little jobs on the side. In an attempt to readjust the balance in favour of such households, it was decided that they should receive 25 per cent of the plots of land which they had contributed to the co-operative. This soon put things right.

In 1964 I again achieved a surplus of a ton. If we hadn't had so many children, and if my wife hadn't been so busy at home, we might have done even better. But by that time she had three to look after, which meant she couldn't spend so long in the fields. Early in 1965 we had our fourth child, another girl. The baby was only five months old when my wife got killed in an air raid. She perished in the American attack on the market at Van Dinh. The market was at the foot of the dam, about seventy yards from the bridge. The American planes came and bombed the bridge, the dam and the market. They destroyed the Thanh Am bridge, they hit the dam; the earth at the foot of the dam buried the people in and around the market. At the time it happened, the market wasn't very busy. My wife was delivering two basketfuls of maize. She was buried alive. More than thirty people died that morning, either buried alive or decapitated. Charred bodies, scraps of flesh, severed arms and severed legs: all these were found dangling from the branches of the trees along the roadside. As soon as I heard the bombs, I got my bike out and cycled to the market as fast as I could – it's about two and a half miles from here. The earth was piled so high that there was no chance of getting the body out at first. I borrowed a pick and started digging. I dug and dug, crying all the time, but I could find no trace of her. However, round about noon the following day the earth-level subsided through the efforts of the workers repairing the dam; and so I was able to recover her body at last. On the first day I searched from seven in the morning till nine at night. I didn't eat a thing, and I didn't pack up and go home until it was too dark to see. I returned at first light the following day. This time

I paddled and swam in the surrounding pools, thinking I might find her there. I fished out several other bodies, but not my wife's. I went on searching the pools until eight in the morning. Eventually I gave up. I just trudged about, letting my legs guide me. And suddenly I found her. She was covered with a thin layer of soil, and her hair was jutting out. I spotted her gold ear-rings and recognized them at once. None of her jewellery was missing. It was the same with all the other bodies: nothing had been stolen. There were no wounds on her body, but her face was swollen to an enormous size and black from suffocation. On the evening of the first day I had found her baskets (though there was no sign of her yoke), together with the nylon thing she used to wear when it was raining; and from then on I had known for certain that she was dead. She lay face-down on her belly, still clutching the yoke. She was thirty-seven. Her clothes were in good condition, but the smell was horrible by that time.

The security officials were there, compiling a report on the raid. I wasn't allowed to take away the ear-rings or the money she had on her. I came back to the co-operative and was given a coffin to bury her in. There were only two victims in the whole of this village. On the first day, the body of a male member of the co-operative was found; on the second, my wife's. The co-operative sent a party of fifteen workers to collect the bodies and escort them back to the village; they were wheeled home on a barrow.

Having to look after the baby girl created a lot of difficulties for me. On the co-operative's recommendation, we were provided with coupons entitling us to four tins of milk a month. The next few months were very hard. My mother-in-law looked after the youngest child, and I looked after the others. We had a terrible feeling of sadness and hatred. My children used to cry every day at the thought of their mother; and I cried too, as if I had lost an arm. That year we were short of rice. We were six hundredweights short, so the co-operative gave us some. In 1966 we were five and a half hundredweights short, and once again the co-operative made up the difference. This year I have reduced the deficit to three hundredweights. The co-operative has made it good, and so we have enough to live on. We're a family of seven: my mother-in-law, the five children and myself. I'm the only one engaged in productive work. My eldest daughter is still at school. She is in Class 5, the boy is in Class 3, and the second eldest girl is in Class 1. The other two are too small for nursery school yet; they'll go next year. I'm too old to join the army and seek revenge for my wife's death. Instead, I work hard and produce as much as I can — firstly to provide for our needs, and secondly as a contribution to the fight against aggression. Whenever my children cry, I think of the crime the Americans have committed and feel full of hatred towards them. The worst feeling of all comes when a child is unwell. I get a strangling sensation in my heart and I long for vengeance, remembering how hard I've had to struggle to make ends meet and what a rough time my children have been through.

4. The Province of Nin Binh

Tram Tinh, aged forty-seven, permanent member of the Party Committee for the province of Nin Binh, and permanent member of the Provincial Administrative Committee:

Our province has 530,000 inhabitants. It covers an area of 480 square miles and is divided into six districts and a provincial capital. Our province is essentially agricultural. It contains 123 villages. Industry has only begun to develop here in the past few years. Before the revolution in August 1945, the inhabitants were condemned to a life of want. The soil was in the hands of the French settlers, the landowners and the Church. These groups controlled 70 per cent of the arable land. There were thirty-six concessions belonging to French settlers. In the early months of 1945 we suffered a great many deaths as a result of famine. In the district of Kuim Senh, 20,000 people died of starvation. On assuming power, we confiscated the settlers' lands and shared them out among the peasants at the rate of a quarter of an acre per head. Not a single inhabitant has died of starvation since independence.

Then came the Catholic exodus to the South, prompted by such propaganda as: 'The revolutionary government is out to liquidate the Catholic religion' or 'God and Christ have moved to the South'. This kind of talk persuaded a number of Catholics to leave the North. Few of those who left belonged to the working class: the majority were rich people and well-off peasants.

In July 1961 a C47 dropped a commando group over the coastal region. The plane was brought down by our militia and we captured the troops. In June 1963 the Americans dispatched some more commandos to the village of Khanh Cuong, in the district of Yen Khanh. That was on 7 June 1963. These four commandos were all captured. On 22 May 1965 our province suffered its first air raid. Escalation intensified between May and December 1965: we were raided five or six times a month. In 1966 the American attacks became heavier and more numerous, occurring on nearly twenty days in every month. Ninety-eight villages were bombed. The provincial capital was completely flattened, and so were two rural centres. They destroyed churches, pagodas, temples, community centres, dikes, floodgates, schools, hospitals. . . . There were very few military objectives among all these. On 24 April 1966 they attacked Chu Chung. Seventy-six people were killed, including thirty-six women and about thirty children. They attacked the provincial capital daily from 13 to 19 September 1966, dropping hundreds of bombs. During one raid on the village of Minh Than, in September 1966, the Americans dropped 127 bombs. Many villages were annihilated – Hoa Loc, for instance. They also attacked our dams and dikes in July 1966, at the height of the flood season. On 7 July they carried out two raids on the dike at the village of Khanh Thiem.

In 1966 they attacked our dikes twenty-nine times. In 1967 they have attacked the dikes and the irrigation system twenty times. Thirteen churches were destroyed and nine schools bombed in 1966. The total figures for 1967 are not yet available, of course; but so far – with three months still to go – seven schools and four churches have been bombed. In 1966 twelve hospitals and medical units were destroyed. All our roads and bridges have been bombed, but the Americans have failed to paralyse our communications. They make things difficult for us, but we keep the wheels turning. If a bridge is destroyed, we put up a couple of temporary bridges in its place. They have also made use of their navy and bombarded our coastline. They have damaged a number of villages, but generally speaking we have managed to limit the loss of human lives by digging carefully planned systems of trenches, shelters and individual dugouts. By the way, in addition to military attacks they sometimes carry out psychological attacks, dropping leaflets, children's toys, transistor radios, clothes, pens and pencils. When this happens, we gather them all together and burn them. They drop toys, and then the very next day they come back and drop bombs. However, life goes on. . . . We have set up home-guard units all over the province. Most of the members are youngsters. They see plenty of active service. Fifty-five American planes have been brought down over the province. Of these, the home-guard units can claim four.

In the sphere of agricultural production, our figures show an improvement of 227 per cent over those for 1939. At that time the level of rice production stood at twenty-three hundred-weights per hectare. In 1965 we achieved two and a half tons, and we are now approaching four tons. 1965 brought an improvement of 8.63 per cent over 1964, and 1966 brought a further improvement of 1.8 per cent. In the industrial sphere we did 17.7 per cent better than in 1964. Our plan is to develop regional industry so that eventually we shall be self-sufficient. We have a factory producing machine-tools and agricultural machinery. We have an electrical repair works and a factory turning out 5,000 tons of phosphate manure a year. We have a cement works with the same annual output – 5,000 tons – a chemical works, and a coalmine producing anthracite. We have a small pickling factory, a sugar refinery, a pottery and a glass-works. We have cigarette factories, too.

In addition to rice, we grow rush for industrial uses. We make mats with it. Rush has given rise to a whole handicrafts industry. We also grow tobacco, coffee, groundnuts, soya and haricot beans. As for livestock, we breed pigs, goats and buffaloes, which are now somewhat increasing in number. Fish-breeding is enjoying great success. We also – I forgot to mention this – have a factory manufacturing river craft.

In spite of the war, we are carrying out three revolutions at once: a revolution in productivity, which we are trying to bring to a peak; a technical revolution, in the agricultural as well as the industrial sphere; and finally an ideological and cultural revolution. In the cultural sphere, we in this province had an illiteracy rate of 95 per cent in 1945; only 4,000 pupils received primary education in the days of the French. By 1958, illiteracy had been overcome throughout the province. In 1965 we had 130,000 pupils attending first-, second- and third-phase schools. This year we have more than 140,000. We have ten third-phase schools, and 70 per cent of the villages have their own second-phase schools. As for public health, there used to be only one hospital; today there are eight. Every district has its own hospital, every village its own medical unit and maternity centre. We have thirty doctors, fifty medical auxiliaries, fifty pharmacists and 300 nurses and orderlies working in our hospitals, not to mention those employed in the villages. Sixty per cent of our villages have a medical auxiliary in charge of the local unit. The district hospitals deal with cases which previously had to be sent to the provincial hospital, and the provincial hospital carries out operations which were previously only performed in Hanoi. We have ten mobile cinema teams and three professional artistic groups; there is an amateur group in every village. We still do our best to provide people with culture and relaxation, in spite of these difficult times, for it is important that people should be entertained and that life should continue as normally as possible.

Naturally there are a great many difficulties. Travel is difficult. Most journeys have to be made by night. The raids don't help. Schools have had to be evacuated. The provincial hospital (500 beds) has been totally destroyed; so it, too, has had to be evacuated and decentralized. Our people say we do not enjoy the freedom of our own skies, but we don't grumble: we realize that we are getting no more than our share of the raids, and that things are far worse in the vicinity of the seventeenth and eighteenth parallels. We are quite convinced that we shall hold out. As the raids intensify, so production increases. The more often the Americans come, the harder we work. But I don't suppose it occurs to them that they are stimulating production.

Nguyen Thi La, aged twenty, militiawoman:

Our unit was founded on 17 May 1967. The Village Administrative Committee sent us on a five-day training course. The purpose of the course was to teach us how to fire a rifle and a machine-gun. The Executive Committee was anxious that we should learn to shoot well, and we were aware of our responsibilities. We are physically small and the weapons were clumsy great things; but we were keen to learn, and morale is what really matters. At the end of the five days we were fully trained. The provincial military command and the district military command supplied us with three automatic weapons for use against aircraft. We also had a few rifles. We have kept these weapons in good condition since the day they were handed to us. We were impatient to do battle with the American planes. We were delighted at being given these automatic weapons, and we looked around for suitable spots to dig trenches and erect fortifications.

On 6 June 1967 we had our first encounter with American planes. We didn't shoot any of them down, but the clash provided us with our baptism of fire. The American bombs exploded within a hundred yards of us. We didn't budge, though, for we were intent on improving our aim. Two days later we were involved in a second duel. We didn't claim any victims that time either. We analysed this second encounter and realized where we had gone wrong: we had been under-shooting. The planes had fired and missed too, but at least they had managed to drop their bombs within a hundred yards of us. On 16 June two more planes appeared in the sky. The first dropped six bombs, but we didn't open fire. We waited for the second. It dived to 2,500 feet, and at that point we sat up and took notice. When it was safely in our sights, as big as a pumpkin, we opened fire with all three machine-guns, scoring seventeen hits. The guns are Russian-built 12 x 7s. Our platoon was posted in four combat positions that day. The plane burst into flames as soon as it was hit. It came down nine miles away, and we went off in search of the wreckage. It was an A4B. Everyone in the neighbourhood had seen the plane catch fire. The provincial commander and district commander came and congratulated us, and so did the members of the Administrative Committee. Our platoon has been very popular ever since, and our ambition now is to shoot down another plane and capture the crew alive. The truth is, we hate the American aircrews with all our hearts – for they come here and destroy our villages, they destroy the roads we have built, they destroy all the results of the years and years of work.

Do Thi Dan, peasant, aged forty-two. Her stone house is surrounded with banked-up walls of earth, to protect it from dispersal bombs. There is a trench under the three beds. Holy pictures are displayed on a small altar. The room also contains several Party newspapers. On the walls are photographs of President Ho, General Giap, Pham Van Dong – the Prime Minister – and Truong Chinh:

I'm a Catholic, and the mother of seven children. The eldest is fifteen and the youngest a year. I was orphaned at fifteen. My parents hadn't any land of their own. We used to go to market with my mother and help her with the buying and selling. My father was an agricultural labourer.

I went into service, working for a family of rich peasants. I got married in 1946, when I was twenty-one. My husband was the landowner's manservant, and we managed to save enough to buy a small house. My husband didn't own any land either, and both of us had to work as day-labourers. In 1955 we received about a mau under the land reform programme. My husband became a member of the mutual-aid labour pool, and we borrowed enough money from the state to buy a buffalo. After that, collective farming began. In addition to working for the co-operative, I bred pigs. From 1960 to 1964 I sold the state over two hundredweights of pork a year, an average of three pigs a year. I keep poultry, too – about thirty birds. I joined the co-operative in 1960, and from then until 1964 I sold between fourteen hundredweights and a ton of rice a year. I kept 2.4 tons for my family, and the rest went to the state. In 1965 and 1966 the harvests were better: I kept 2.8 tons for my family and sold 1.2 tons to the state. The work of the co-operative is carried out by production groups, and I am a full-time member of a group. I work six days a week, all the year round. I still breed pigs and poultry: at present I have five pigs, including one sow, and thirty birds. I'm quite well off, for I also have an orchard where I grow orange trees and vegetables. The pigs bring me in a profit of 200 dongs, and I make another 400 from the rice I sell to the state. The pay we receive from the co-operative depends on how much work we put in, but my husband and I make over 200 dongs between us.

Altogether we have about 800 dongs coming in every year, and with that we can afford to buy clothes, pave the yard and make improvements about the house. I've deposited 500 dongs in the village savings bank.

Our village has escaped bombing so far, but there have been raids all round us. This makes everyday life difficult. The raids interrupt the work in the fields. Since the end of 1965 we have dug a trench inside the house and erected a wall to protect us against dispersal bombs. The shelter offers complete protection and has an escape exit leading to the garden. We built it at the suggestion of the Management Committee and the head of the local militia. In spite of the aggression, our standard of living is rising. There is certainly a great difference between things as they are now and things as they used to be in the days of the French colonialists. Before, we were living aimlessly; now we have hopes for the future.

My main hope is that we shall drive the Americans out and reap bigger harvests and earn a better living, with nothing to disturb our peace. I hope all my children go on with their schooling so that in time they may become skilled workers or technicians within the ranks of the co-operative.

The Hamlet of Huong Dao
in the district of Phat Diem

Vu Van Cat, peasant, aged sixty. With him is his youngest son, aged five, whose leg has had to be amputated as the result of an air raid:

I was born in the village of Thong Kiem, in the district of Kim Son – not far from here. I'm a Catholic. Under the French I didn't have any land at all, except for the tiny plot my hut stood on. I had a few birds and a pair of pigs, but no oxen. My parents were poor and used to work for a landowner. By the time I was twelve, I was minding buffalo. When I was sixteen, and therefore more or less grown-up, I became a hired labourer on a landowner's estate. At twenty-five I married a fellow-Catholic. Shortly afterwards I left the landowner's employment.

I had to do jobs for several landowners at once. I was paid in rice. I have fathered nine children. When I was a child myself, back in colonial times, living conditions were very hard. Every year, I used to run deeper into debt with the landowner. In those days we were all subject to the capitation tax. I also had to pay a tax on my house, and other money besides. Some years it was very hard to pay the tax, and you had to borrow. The landowner used to lend money at an extortionate rate. On a loan of ten piastres, you had to pay two and a half piastres' interest a month. A piastre a month was the very least you could expect to pay. There used to be a saying: 'Borrowing cuts a man's throat.' There were some wealthy men in the village. The landowner I'm speaking of had nearly ninety acres of paddy-fields. He was rich and he had power. He was a Catholic and was well in with the hierarchy. He lived in clover. At least he didn't beat us, though – unlike *some* of the local landlords. Here in the village, it was the mayor who took decisions in the old days. He was elected by the elders. I used to be illiterate. I can read now, though not very quickly.

I've been to Hanoi a few times; it's fifty miles from here. I used to go there looking for work – but I never found any, so I came back. I really love my village. Once I spent twelve days in Hanoi, looking for work. I was like a fish out of water. It was all bustle and tear, and I soon felt homesick. Luckily I met a friend from the village. I was so glad to see him! We came back home together.

The famine of 1945 caused a great many deaths in the village, but I had a fishing boat and was able to sell what I caught and buy rice. That was how I managed to keep body and soul together. Afterwards I went back to working on the land. From 1945 until 1949 there were official schemes to help us find work. I used to deliver rice and other goods by sampan, and this added a little to my earnings. I also worked as a carpenter's mate. That was how I earned my living during the war of resistance. I didn't have any dealings with the puppet administration.

With the return of peace in 1954–5, I received nearly a mau under the land reform programme. I became a member of the mutual-aid labour pool: this was a form of collective labour which operated before the farming co-operative was set up. In 1956 I bought a buffalo. Things were looking up for me: for the first time in my life I owned land and a buffalo. In 1959 the collective farming scheme was introduced. I joined the co-operative. In my first year of membership I earned enough to cover my basic needs and pay off my debts. By 1960 the children of my first marriage were old enough to work for their living. Only one of them is still alive: he lives on his own now. The others are my children by my second wife; she is a Catholic too. They are still only young. The older boy is ten, and this one is the baby. Look what they've done to him! Up to 1964, my family had an income of 350 pounds of rice per head per year. I had two male pigs and a sow and a dozen birds and a small private allotment in which I grew taros and other vegetables.

The co-operative is made up of eleven production groups, and each group has about a hundred members. There are nearly a thousand of us in all. My own group consists of sixty workers. It is the production group which allocates work to the individual co-operator. There is a management committee of fifteen members, elected by general ballot. I'm not on the committee myself. I'm just an ordinary co-operator.

I go to church every Sunday, and all my children have been baptized. I go to Confession: the new regime guarantees freedom of religious faith. About a third of the villagers here are Catholics. We are divided into Catholic wards. In 1961 I was deputy chief of a ward. One of my sons has married a Catholic, the others are too young to marry yet. I have only three children left. Six were killed in an air raid on 2 November 1966, and this one – the youngest – lost a leg. My second wife got killed as well.

Before the attacks started, we never managed to produce two tons an acre; but we have reached that figure now. We are hoping this year's harvest will show even better results. We are not short of any of the basic necessities. I get three yards of clothing material a year, I get salt, I get oil. There may sometimes be a delay in receiving certain items, but we receive them in the end. My house was destroyed, and with the co-operative's help I have been able to build a smaller one for myself and the surviving children. There are air-raid warnings nearly every day. When we hear them we take shelter, then get on with our work. Production does not suffer.

The Americans are cruel, very cruel. They are out to conquer our country so that they can rule it in their own way. Already they are in the South, and beyond any doubt they mean to invade us from the skies. Sooner or later they will be beaten, though. What is socialism? If you ask me, socialism is a way of improving the lives of the peasants.

The Village of Luu Phuong

Nguyen The Hoi, militiawoman, aged twenty-eight:

My mother is still alive. My father died in the famine of 1945. He was a landless peasant and used to work for a landowner. I have one brother. My family were not natives of this village: they came from a neighbouring district. We were evacuated during the first war of resistance. When peace returned, we received a grant of land and took over the house of some Catholics who had moved to Thanh Hoa, in the South. My brother was able to go to school, but I was ten and had to help my mother and work in the fields. I managed to get some schooling later, though, and am now up to Class 6 standard. In 1956 I attended supplementary classes, but played no part in political and social activities. In 1959 I began to participate in local social activities, and in 1961 I was one of the first to join the militia. In 1955 we all received grants of land under the land reform programme. My family was given a mau. In 1956 I joined the mutual-aid labour pool and became one of the organizers.

After the co-operative was set up, I became deputy chief of a production group. I do the same jobs as the other co-operators: ploughing, harrowing, pricking out, harvesting.... Quite recently, in August 1967, I became a Party member. I give orders to men and women, and they do as I ask because it was they who elected me to lead them. For heads of production groups are elected by general ballot, like the members of the Management Committee. In 1962 I was posted away from the village and spent a year working with a military training unit at Kim Dai, five miles from where I lived. These American raids have caused production difficulties. The paddy-fields are two and a half miles from the camp, and the journey has to be made on foot each day. This wastes a lot of time, for the paddy-fields are not concentrated in one spot – they are scattered far and wide. There are thirty-two people in my unit. Before the air attacks started, our whole effort was concentrated on production. Today, sixteen of us work in the fields – one in two. Of the other sixteen, ten are on twenty-four-hour call to repel raiders, three ferry the sampans back and forth, and three do the washing and cooking. In spite of these difficulties it is essential that we should step up production, and we have managed to do so. Previously we were reaping 1.6 tons an acre; in 1966 we reaped two tons. Our production techniques are improving, especially as regards the use of fertilizers, but the main reason for the increase is the high morale that stems from resisting aggression.

To date, my unit has shot down four enemy aircraft. Actually, one of the four was destroyed in collaboration with the army. The first was an F100; the second, on 19 August 1966, an H4T; the third – that was the one we shared with the regular army— on 2 January 1967; the fourth, on 6 August 1967, an F4H. The first was brought down by rifle fire and took only twenty-seven bullets. The second was brought down by rifle fire, too. We got the third with a machine-gun, and the fourth with rifles and Stens. It was flying at about 2,500 feet. The time was 7 a.m. Six American aircraft approached from the south-east, flying in pairs. As the pair in the centre flew overhead, the unit commander said: 'Prepare to fire.' We were all ready and waiting. 'Fire!' he shouted. We had five rifles and two Sten-guns. We fired. The plane made off, trailing a column of yellow smoke. The right wing was damaged, and suddenly – quite a while afterwards – it crashed. The victory was announced over the radio.

There is certainly complete equality between men and women today. I'm not married, but when I do get married I shall choose my own husband. True, men and women were officially equal even before the attacks started. But the spirit which women have shown under fire has won them far more respect than they enjoyed before. Men's attitudes have changed.

Conclusion

The Role of Ideology

I have endeavoured in this book to explain the reasons for the exceptional powers of resistance shown by the people of North Vietnam. I began by looking at the matter from an historical standpoint, for the specific conditions which the country has inherited are of no minor importance. Then I examined it from the point of view of the social and economic organization which stems from a particular ideology, for here was another vital factor. Yet these explanations would remain inadequate if reference were not made, however briefly, to the special role which that ideology fulfils.

The personal accounts given in the preceding pages contain a wealth of sociological material which I have left the reader to analyse for himself. But I will now venture to point out that many of the remarks made by officials reflect the 'voluntaristic' ideology which characterizes the Leninist attitudes of the Vietnamese Workers' Party. Similarly, the ordinary peasants – men and women alike – show a continual preoccupation with *producing*, which they see as a sure way of bolstering national independence.

Revolutionary ideology, except when patently at variance with the facts (e.g. the existence of wholesale corruption or poor economic planning), does more than instil the capacity to transform patterns of production; it gives rise to the possibility of altering people's attitudes and mental habits – in short, the ethics of an entire community. It is not, as is sometimes claimed, a question of a new breed of man emerging, but of masses being transformed through active participation in a struggle in which they have a genuine stake.

In the South, the disintegration of the Diem regime – and more recently of the governments headed by Air Marshal Ky and General Thieu – confirm, if confirmation were needed, that historical circumstances are not in themselves sufficient to account for the present. True, one of the features of Vietnamese civilization is an exceptional aptitude for collective action; but it is through a revolutionary struggle based on agrarian demands and a sense of national dignity that the N L F has captured the support and imagination of the peasants of South Vietnam.

In the North, the leaders of revolutionary thought have successfully adapted the tool of Marxism-Leninism to national conditions, while at the same time transforming the latter. The regime opened the door to enlightenment by completely altering the existing patterns of production; but it also provided the masses with an ideology which would modify their attitude to work even before the economic conditions were fundamentally changed. In those countries which until recently ranked as colonies or near-colonies, such a transformation would seem – in the light of various experiments on the three continents – unachievable except by the use of the ideological tool wrought from scientific socialism; for this alone can forge the link between a given situation and the ideas and watchwords which are capable of transforming them.

Hanoi, October 1967 – Paris, June 1968

Select Bibliography

Burchett, W. G., *The Furtive War*, International Publishers, New York, 1965.

Burchett, W. G., *Vietnam: Inside Story of the Guerrilla War*, International Publishers, New York, 1965.

Devillers, P., *Histoire du Vietnam de 1940 à 1952*, Editions du Seuil, Paris, 3rd ed., 1952.

Devillers, P., and Lacouture, J., *End of a War: Indochina 1954*, Pall Mall Press, London, 1969.

Fall, B. B., *The Viet-Minh*, Pall Mall Press, London, Praeger, New York, rev. ed., 1965.

Fall, B. B., *The Two Viet-Nams*, Pall Mall Press, London, Praeger, New York, rev. ed. 1965.

Fall, B. B., *Vietnam Witness*, Pall Mall Press, London, Praeger, New York, 1966.

Gettleman, M. (ed.), *Vietnam (History, Documents and Opinions . . .)*, Fawcett, New York, 1965, Penguin Books, London, 1966.

General Giap, *Big Victory, Great Talk*, Pall Mall Press, London, 1968.

Gourou, P., *Les paysans du Delta Tonkinois*, P. Hartmann, Paris, 1936.

Hammer, E. J., *The Struggle for Indochina*, Stanford University Press, California, rev. ed., 1966.

Hickey, G. C., *Village in Vietnam*, Yale University Press, 1964.

Lacouture, J., *Le Vietnam entre deux paix*, Editions du Seuil, Paris, 1965.

Lancaster, D., *The Emancipation of French Indo-China*, O.U.P. for R.I.I.A., London, 1961.

Le Chau, *Le Vietnam socialiste*, F. Maspero, Paris, 1966.

McCarthy, Mary, *Vietnam*, Harcourt Brace, New York, Weidenfeld and Nicolson, London, 1967, Penguin Books, London, 1968.

Mus, P., *Vietnam: Sociologie d'une Guerre*, Editions du Seuil, Paris, 1952.

Nguyen Kien, *Le Sud-Vietnam depuis Dien Bien Phu*, F. Maspero, Paris, 1963.

Partisans, Special number, January-February 1968, 'Le peuple vietnamien et la guerre'.

Pike, Douglas C., *The Vietcong: Organization and Technique of the NLF of South Vietnam*, Massachusetts Institute of Technology Press, 1966.

Schurmann, Franz, *The Politics of Escalation in Vietnam*, Beacon Press, Boston, 1966.

Zagoria, Donald, *Vietnam Triangle*, Pegasus, New York, 1967.

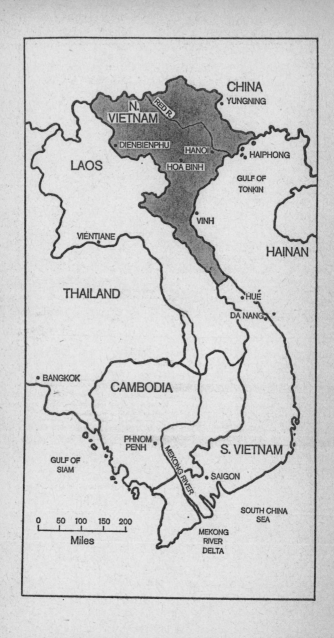

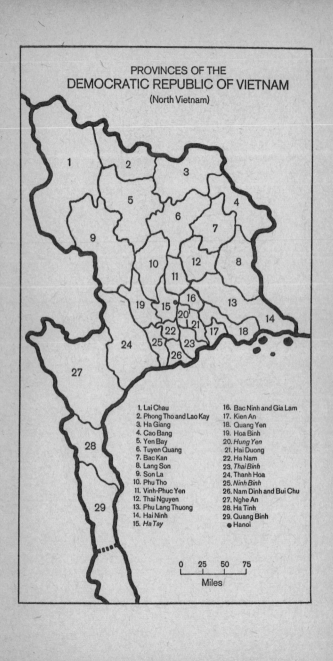

PROVINCES OF THE
DEMOCRATIC REPUBLIC OF VIETNAM
(North Vietnam)

1. Lai Chau
2. Phong Tho and Lao Kay
3. Ha Giang
4. Cao Bang
5. Yen Bay
6. Tuyen Quang
7. Bac Kan
8. Lang Son
9. Son La
10. Phu Tho
11. Vinh-Phuc Yen
12. Thai Nguyen
13. Phu Lang Thuong
14. Hai Ninh
15. *Ha Tay*
16. Bac Ninh and Gia Lam
17. Kien An
18. Quang Yen
19. Hoa Binh
20. *Hung Yen*
21. Hai Duong
22. Ha Nam
23. *Thai Binh*
24. Thanh Hoa
25. *Ninh Binh*
26. Nam Dinh and Bui Chu
27. Nghe An
28. Ha Tinh
29. Quang Binh
● Hanoi

```
0    25    50    75
```
Miles

Some other books published by Penguins are described
on the following pages.

Civilian Resistance as a National Defence

Non-violent Action against Aggression

Edited by Adam Roberts

After Russia's brutal invasion of Czechoslovakia it became clear that many civilian activities (including radio and press) had been successfully, if spontaneously, deployed to resist the invader.

We now have to ask ourselves whether a nation can defend itself effectively against armed attack by non-violent means. Can civil disobedience, strikes, boycotts, underground newspapers and the whole armoury of passive resistance be expanded and co-ordinated into a strategy of national defence, with patriotic government running in parallel with enemy or puppet authority? Many experts believe they can.

This prophetic book was published (as *The Strategy of Civilian Defence*) before the Czech crisis. Its distinguished contributors include Sir Basil Liddell Hart, the foremost military writer of our time; Alun Gwynne Jones, now Lord Chalfont and a Minister of State at the Foreign Office; and such North American experts as Thomas C. Schelling and Lt-Col. D. J. Goodspeed. They see civilian defence, not as a soft option, like pacifism, but as perhaps the best answer to physical attack, the *coup d'état* or the imposition of totalitarian rule. The editor's new introduction describing the Czech resistance to Soviet occupation confirms that the similarity between the theories in this book and the practice of the Czechs was rightly called (by Brian Connell on the B.B.C.) 'absolutely uncanny'.

'A thoughtful book, of uniformly high quality'—*Listener*

South-East Asia in Turmoil

Brian Crozier

For years South-East-Asia has been the political fisherman's paradise. Its troubled waters have seen western imperialism, eastern nationalism, comintern agitation, Japanese occupation, Sino-Soviet conflict, American intervention, and the explosive ambitions of the local boy, Dr Sukarno. To the eye of the non-specialist the whole area presents a bewildering blur.

Brian Crozier has managed to assemble the myriad pieces of this jig-saw puzzle – Laos, Vietnam, Sarawak, Brunei, Hatta, Sihanouk, Ho Chi Minh, Bao Dai, and all the others – into a continuous and coherent narrative. In *South-East Asia in Turmoil* he examines Soviet, Chinese, American, British, and French policies, explains where they went wrong, and suggests future courses of action.

South-East Asia is a political volcano today. Any reader who is looking for a thread through the labyrinth of violent news from there will do well to read this book, which lays out clearly who has done what . . . where . . . and why.

'Never dull . . . blessedly free from semantic confusion . . . very fairly gives us facts; he seldom gives opinions' – Graham Greene in the *New Statesman*

The Cultural Revolution in China

Joan Robinson

Most western journalists see China lurching to self-destruction in an orgy of random violence, mad adulation, inexplicable jargon and meticulous, meaningless ritual. How, they ask, can the Red Guards believe their own wall posters? What is the meaning of a 'party person in authority taking the capitalist road'? And how can the Thoughts of Mao make crops grow on a stony hill?

In this documentary investigation the author calls upon the Chinese themselves to explain their revolution. Joan Robinson, Professor of Economics at Cambridge and author of the Pelican *Economic Philosophy*, has recently visited China. From conversations, reported here, and from the key documents, which have never before been published in the West, she focuses attention on the phenomenon most puzzling to those outside China – a ruler so hostile to his own administration that he incites and leads a nation-wide popular revolution against it.

The Biafra Story

Frederick Forsyth

In Nigeria we are witnessing 'the biggest bloodbath in Africa's history'. Civil war had been in progress for a year when photographic evidence of the murder and starvation of women and children and the destruction of villages began to appear in the British press in 1968: today the assault on Biafra begins to look like genocide.

What are the historical, military, political, and economic factors which have added up to this ghastly picture of a small nation fighting with its back to the wall? In this Penguin Special an experienced journalist, writing from an unashamedly Biafran point of view, traces the origins of the civil war to its roots in tribal antagonisms and British colonial policy. He describes the two 'coups' of 1966 and the provocations that led up to Biafra's secession in May, 1967; in his account of the war's progress he shows how attempts to relieve starvation in Biafra have been frustrated at every turn and how the so-called 'peace conferences' were no more than empty charades.

The Biafra Story, in short, is a shocking indictment of the military clique which controls the Nigerian Federal Government and of the Labour Government which has consistently supported it, not least with arms.

Abuse of Power

U.S. Foreign Policy from Cuba to Vietnam

Theodore Draper

This short critique by a distinguished American historian is more weighty than several volumes of conventional moral indignation. Stage by stage, in a disquietingly effective argument, Theodore Draper proves that in Vietnam, as in the past in Cuba and Dominica, America has increasingly relied on military power to salvage political defeat. During the Johnson administration hundreds of thousands of men and millions of tons of munitions were flung into a cockpit of little strategic significance, as a defence mechanism not so much against the communists as against the incursions of reality into American strategic thinking. Dishonesty of thought was accompanied by dishonesty of expression; and in the resultant semantic confusion words have lost all meaning and America has almost stopped taking international politics seriously.

'Not the least merit of Theodore Draper's devastating critique of American policy in Vietnam is that it is also the best concise, compact history of the whole U.S. involvement in South East Asia' – Anthony Howard in the *Observer*

'I do not know of anyone who writes with such care and precision on foreign policy as Theodore Draper' – J. K. Galbraith

Not for sale in the U.S.A. or Canada

Two Studies of Vietnam by Mary McCarthy

Hanoi

'There are many questions one does not want to ask in Hanoi'.

In North Vietnam Mary McCarthy enjoyed the hospitality of a people which her immensely powerful American compatriots were struggling to annihilate. Much of the fascination of this virtuoso piece of reporting springs from her personal and principled reactions to the endurance of the North Vietnamese in the face of circumstances which Western nations would find insufferable. Like her previous volume, *Vietnam*, this book is both a painfully acute, ultimately inspiring account of a resistance which can (without risk of cliché) be called heroic, and an account of an identity crisis afflicting one American intellectual and the whole Western world.

Vietnam

Is this a war that we – or anyone – should support?

In one of the most honest, most heart-rending reports to come out of Vietnam, Mary McCarthy shows America fighting a war it cannot win in a theatre it will not leave.

As she landed at Saigon (now a cheap suburb of the U.S.A.) as she toured villages, camps, hospitals, and schools, as she listened to the glib euphemisms of soldiers, airmen, civilians, and pacifiers, the bombs were dropping and the fires burning.

Every statement by every official invites us to ask: 'Can these men really believe themselves?'

Not for sale in the U.S.A. or Canada.